*"Do you want a 'make-believe' or a 'really truly'?"
grandmother would ask.*

Really Trulies

A Little Book of Verses and True Stories

By

Adelaide Bee Evans

Author of Easy Steps in the Bible Story,
The Bible Year, Strange People
and Customs, etc.

TEACH Services, Inc.
P U B L I S H I N G
www.TEACHServices.com • (800) 367-1844

World rights reserved. This book or any portion thereof may not be copied or reproduced in any form or manner whatever, except as provided by law, without the written permission of the publisher, except by a reviewer who may quote brief passages in a review.

The author assumes full responsibility for the accuracy of all facts and quotations as cited in this book. The opinions expressed in this book are the author's personal views and interpretations, and do not necessarily reflect those of the publisher.

This book is provided with the understanding that the publisher is not engaged in giving spiritual, legal, medical, or other professional advice. If authoritative advice is needed, the reader should seek the counsel of a competent professional.

Facsimile Reproduction

As this book played a formative role in the development of Christian thought and the publisher feels that this book, with its candor and depth, still holds significance for the church today. Therefore the publisher has chosen to reproduce this historical classic from an original copy. Frequent variations in the quality of the print are unavoidable due to the condition of the original. Thus the print may look darker or lighter or appear to be missing detail, more in some places than in others.

Copyright © 2023 TEACH Services, Inc.
ISBN-13: 978-1-4796-1673-2 (Paperback)

Published by

TEACH Services, Inc.
P U B L I S H I N G
www.TEACHServices.com • (800) 367-1844

Dedication

FOR Edith and Junior and Florence Louise, and all the other little boys and girls who "like true stories best," this book was written, and to them it is lovingly given.

Remembering

"Of course I'll remember," said Betty
  (She was almost indignant, indeed)—
"Two cookies, to keep from forgetting
  A package of caraway seed."

But when once before the long counter,
  Our Betty stood telling her need,
She said, "Grandma wants, Mr. Whipple,
  Two cookies of goaway seed."

Preface

Dear Edith and Junior and Florence Louise: A long, long time ago a little girl lived in a tiny brown house in a small village — just such a home as hundreds of girls and boys live in to-day. This little girl liked stories. In the morning when grandmother was shelling peas, she would gladly shell some too, if only grandmother would "tell a story." In the afternoon, when grandmother's fingers were making the shining knitting needles fly, she would bring her low stool and sit where she could look up into dear grandmother's kind face, and ask for "another story." And in the evening when the stars were shining, and she was safely tucked into her small "trundle bed," she would beg for "just one more."

"Do you want a 'make-believe' or a 'really truly'?" grandmother would ask.

"O, a 'really truly,'" the little girl would say; and then grandmother would smile, and begin. She told about the days when she was a little girl, and all about her pet deer. She told, too, how *her* grandmother used to tell stories to *her*, and how she baked the tiniest, roundest, yellowest little cakes on a griddle, all for her, to eat with maple syrup!

Best of all, the little girl liked to hear about the twelve boys and girls, all one family, who were grandmother's cousins, and their pranks and games. There was a certain sad Christmas that came to the twelve. Father and mother went away in the big sleigh to buy the presents; and the children, left at home, did something that they had been told not to do. So though the parents were sorry, there was no Christmas in their house that year. No presents, no tree, no stockings hung up in front of the wide fireplace that seemed just *made* for Christmas stockings! For in those days, children were taught to obey, said grandmother, and to tell the truth. And if they didn't, they were punished.

A great many children like the "really truly" stories best, and that is the reason this little book of "Really Trulies" has been written. It is hoped that the things that happened to these "really truly" boys and girls may be a help to Edith and Junior and Florence Louise, and all the other little boys and girls who "like true stories best," and that in everything they do they will always choose "whatsoever things are *true*."

ADELAIDE BEE EVANS.

The Names of the Stories and Verses in this Book

The Surprise	13
The Stars	18
A Little Girl Who Did Not Like to Ask	21
Her Little Brother	27
Going With Father	29
When Bread Tasted Like Cake	37
Sonny's Bible Promise	45
A Flower Story	50
The Cornucopia	53
Be True, Be Kind	60
True's Money	63
Picking Up Grubs	71
Neighborhood Nuisance or Neighborhood Joy	82
The Blue Cloud	77
Plans	75
Milton's Honan Pledge	83
A Bear Story	89
At Grandma's	95
Fenton's Fall	97
Can You Tell?	102
Modesta's Bible	103
The Locket	109

The Hornets' Nest	115
My Little Brook	119
I'm Sorry	121
The Invitation	125
Tell It to Jesus	127
When Norma Was Lost	133
Whistle, My Lad	137
Saying and Doing	128
Playing Doctor	139
Dolly Must Go to Bed	143
The Picnic	145
Bernice Irene	150
When Jack Said, "No"	151
Brothers	155
Two Pennies	157
The Spring	161
Tobacco	162
The Visit	163
Beth's Happiest Christmas	169
God's Promises	176

Really Trulies

The Surprise

"OH, dear-r," said Gay, who was eight.

"Oh, dear-r-r," said May, who was six.

"Oh, dear-r-r-r," said Ray, who was only four, and didn't know any better.

> "Such a lovely day for play
> For a little girl named Gay,
> And a little girl named May,
> And a little boy named Ray —
> You'll agree it's very queer
> That the only sound I hear
> Is dear-r! dear-r-r! dear-r-r-r!"

said mother. "Now, what is the matter?" she asked.

"We're *tired* of playing," said the children, one after the other.

Mother looked at them and smiled, and of course they all smiled back. It is fun to have

mother smile, because you are pretty sure that the next thing to happen after a smile will be a pleasant thing.

"Let's go over to Austin's Hill, and see if we can't find **red** raspberries enough to fill a five-quart pail," said mother. "If we can, we'll come back and I'll bake the big dripping pan full of shortcake, and we'll have it for a surprise for father when he comes home this evening."

"Goody! Goody! Goody!" shouted the children, and ran to get their tin cups.

It was great fun to go. First they went through "Dell's Lot," where the children often played, just across the village street; then across a long, narrow bridge over a wide river, through a sawmill that made a scary, screeching sound, and up another road with many white pebbles, to Austin's Hill.

There was a house on this hill that had been begun so long ago that it was old and gray now, but it had never been finished. "Why, mother?" asked May. She had heard the story many times, but it was always new to the children, when they saw the old-new house that had never been a home. "And never will be now," the neighbors said.

"Poor old Mr. Austin was young like father once," said mother, and her smiling eyes looked sad as she said it. "He had a wife and three little girls whom he loved very much; and he thought how pleasant it would be to build a fine home for them. But when the house was just as you see it now, the children were all taken very sick and died, and Mr. Austin did not wish to finish the house then. So he and his wife have lived in the little house on the top of the hill ever since."

"Poor Mr. Austin," said the children. "Is that why he likes to have us come and pick berries on his hill?"

"Perhaps so," said mother; "and now we must make our fingers fly. Let's see who has the first cup full."

Six little hands can pick a good many berries when there is to be a "surprise for father," and when mother's white fingers are helping. So it was not long before the five-quart pail was rounded full, and three little mouths were berry stained too.

"I like to pick berries," said May.

"So do I," said Gay.

"Me too, I yike it," said Ray.

They stopped a few minutes to pick some tender wintergreen leaves, then home they went. All the children helped get the supper. Ray picked up chips for the fire that was to bake the shortcake, May set the table, and Gay oiled the big dripping pan in every corner.

"What would I do without such helpers!" smiled mother, and the children smiled too.

There were bread and butter and warm beans on the table when father came home, and kissed them all around twice before they sat down to eat. Father was hungry, and he looked across at mother. May looked down at her plate, and Gay shut her lips very tight, but Ray began to speak "Me too, I yike —"

"Have some bread and beans, Raymond Boy," said mother, who did not wish the surprise told just then.

"Beans!" finished Ray, and Gay and May giggled as they passed their plates.

Father told them all about taking the gray colt over to Portville, and how the Farley's dog had followed the buggy till he was so tired he had to be taken up on the seat. "Poor little fellow, he didn't know any better than to run away from home," said father.

Really Trulies 17

By and by the beans were all eaten, and everyone had had all the bread and butter he wanted.

"Now — mamma!" shouted the children.

"Now — children!" said mother, and she brought out the big shortcake, on the large platter, all brown and crusty and buttered, and covered with delicious crushed berries. There was yellow cream in a pitcher, too.

"Ah-ha! Now I *see*," said father; and he looked very pleased as he said it.

"Are you s'prised?" cried the children, all at once.

"Indeed I am," he said, "and as I suspect you have all had a hand in getting this treat, I'll have to thank you every one! You are the best children a father ever had."

"Mother was in it too," said May.

"Mother thought of it," said Gay.

"Muvver — too — I — yike —"

"Yes, mother too," said father. "Of course, mother too."

"Shortcake!" said Ray

The Stars

THE sun goes down behind the hill,
  The sky is gold and red,
The fields and woods are very still,
And in the meadow by the mill
  The lambs have gone to bed.

I place my hand in father's hand,
  And up and down we walk;
He tells me tales from every land
In words that I can understand;
  Of many things we talk.

And much we like to watch the sky,
  And see the stars peep out,
At first a few, but by and by,
It matters not how hard I try,
  They're more than I can count.

Just as the glow begins to fade,
  Far in the rosy west,
The Evening Star shines soft and bright;
I think I like its golden light
  Of all the stars the best.

And soon the Dipper, big and bright,
    The Polar Star makes plain;
And that's the star whose steady light
Helps sailors guide their ships aright,
    And bring them home again.

The Little Dipper, bent and queer,
    My father shows to me;
Orion's sword and belt are clear,
The twinkling Pleiades appear,
    The Milky Way I see.

And now 'tis time to say good night,
    But first I kneel and pray
That He who made the stars so bright
Will keep me ever in His sight
    And guide me day by day.

"What's the matter, sis?" asked a big boy.

(20)

A Little Girl Who Did Not Like to Ask

"MAY I go, father? May I go? May I —"

"Just a minute, Julia," said father. "If you keep on asking, how can I answer? Yes, you may go, if mother is willing."

So in two minutes Julia was sitting very proud and happy by father in the new buggy, and they were going "up the road" to Aunt Henrietta's. "Down the road" you went to Cousin Rolly's. Julia was very sure she knew the way to both places.

At Aunt Henrietta's the house was small and gray and cosy. Aunt Henrietta was old and plump and kind; sometimes she had blueberries in a wooden bowl — such big *blue* blueberries, with a soft "bloom" on them, like a gray veil. Blueberry pie, Julia would have told you, was the best tasting pie in the world.

Father was going to stop at Aunt Henrietta's

for a few minutes, and then go on up "the Run." Julia might stay to lunch, and then walk home; it was only a mile and a half, and there were houses in sight most of the way.

"Are you sure you want to?" father asked.

Julia was very sure. She liked better than anything to do things all by herself.

So after lunch she walked out of Aunt Henrietta's gate alone. "I know where to go," she had said, when Aunt Henrietta asked if she was sure which way to go. "Of course I won't get lost,— how could I?"

Julia was only five, and she had never gone alone before. Aunt Henrietta was troubled. "I mustn't bother her," she thought; "but when she goes, I'll just keep an eye on her to see she gets headed right."

But something happened to take Aunt Henrietta's mind when Julia started, so she went, just as she wished to go, "all by herself."

She hadn't a speck of doubt about the way. On each side of Aunt Henrietta's house there was another house that looked as much like it as three peas in the same pod, or three June pinks from the same cluster. Julia smelled the spicy fragrance of the pinks she was taking to mother, and loved it.

On she went, her small bare feet patting softly down in the velvet dust of the road. There were pastures, and cows grazing in them. She felt rather anxious over the matter of fences, for she was *so* afraid of cows. She didn't know why — she just was. But the fences were all right; there didn't seem to be any dogs, either. She liked it just as well if there were no dogs.

It seemed rather a long way. But by and by she came to the wide bridge — and there was a footbridge, too. The first thing you did when you started "up the road" from Julia's house was to walk over a footbridge, if you were going afoot. If you were riding, you crossed the wide bridge. Sometimes Julia wondered why there were two. Perhaps it was the fashion, in that place, to have a bridge for horses and wagons, and another for people.

Anyway, there were the two bridges. But — Julia rubbed her eyes. There *should* be, on one side, the footbridge side, her own little brown house, with mother looking "up the road," and "Deede" standing at the gate. And across there would be "Dell's Lot," where she and Deede often "played house" under the trees.

But *no.* There was a house, but it was on the

wrong side of the road! The footbridge was on the wrong side, too. It was confusing. The house was dirty-white, and pigs ran about in the yard. It couldn't be — it wasn't — home! Instead of "Dell's Lot," on the other side there was only a scrubby hill, covered with scraggly pine trees.

Julia rubbed her eyes again. She couldn't see very well, somehow. And the first thing she knew, the tears were running down her hot, dusty little cheeks.

"What's the matter, sis?" asked a big boy who came over the bridge, to see what was going on.

If there was anything that Julia did *not* like, it was being called "sis," but this was no time to think of trifles.

"I want to go home," she sobbed.

"Well, why don't you go, then?" asked the boy. He wasn't a very polite boy, you see.

"I *was* going home," said Julia, stoutly. "I *was*, and I came to the big bridge, and the little bridge, and — the house, — it isn't *my* house!" More tears came, in spite of herself.

"What's your name?" asked the boy.

"Julia Rose."

"Julia Rose *what?*"

"Benson."

"So you're Mr. Benson's little girl, are you? Your father went past this morning. But you are headed the wrong way, if you want to go home. You turn straight around and follow your nose, and you'll come to the place where you live all right."

To Julia, patting along in the burning dust of that hot afternoon, it seemed as if the road grew longer and longer. She wanted to stop at Aunt Henrietta's, and get a drink of cold water and a piece of bread and butter, but someway she couldn't make herself go inside. Instead, she scooted past the gate as fast as she could, hoping no one would see her.

On and on. How hot and dusty and tired she was! Her feet ached. Her head ached. There was such an empty feeling inside, too. But by and by there was the "Wes Smith house," and beyond it the house where Clara Van Wormer lived, all stately and tall with its white tower and green blinds. Then, the red house where Mrs. Gleason lived, and just a little way farther on the *other* big bridge, and the *other* little bridge, and the small brown house *in the right place*, and mother standing on the porch, and Deede at the gate!

"My dear child!" said mother. "Tell me all about it."

So Julia told her all about it. That she wouldn't ask the way, about the long walk, and the turned-around bridges, and everything.

"My dear child," said mother again. And she washed Julia's face and hands and bathed her feet, and gave her a drink, and a bowl of bread and milk, and held her on her lap while she ate it.

And that was the last Julia remembered that day.

But there was something that she did remember — something she learned "*all by herself*,"— and that was that it is better to ask and be right, than not to ask and be wrong.

That little lesson she never forgot.

Her Little Brother

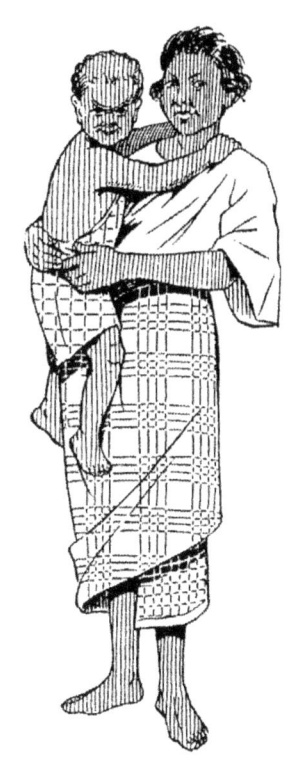

ONE day I stopped, in far Luzon,
   To rest beneath a mango's shade,
And there, dressed in her festal best,
   I met a smiling, brown-skinned maid.

Upon her hip she held the weight
   (For such is custom in that land)
Of sturdy Pablo, three years old,
   Who wept when urged alone to stand.

"How old are you, my child?" I asked,
   "And do you go to school each day?"
"I am eleben, ma'am," she said,
   "This year at home I always stay."

"But why?" again I asked, half vexed
   (So bright was she, so dear, so sweet);
"My mother, ma'am, she's dead, and I
   Must stay to make all clean and neat.

"My sister, Elena Marie,
    Has all my books and school desk too;
I have no time to study now,
    At home there is so much to do."

"This child is old enough to walk,
    To carry him will make you ill."
"That's true, ma'am, but," she softly said,
    "He is my little brother still."

Dear brown-skinned maid of far Luzon,
    Yours is a wisdom from above,—
Pure, peaceable, of gentle rule,
    The wisdom of unselfish love.

Going With Father

An I-tin-er-a-ting Journey, No. 1

FLORENCE has lived in China all her life except once when she went to "America-on-a-furlough." You see, her father and mother are missionaries, and after they have stayed seven years in China, they may go home a year to rest, and to see their own folks, and to eat lettuce and celery and fresh fruit without cooking or scalding, and to drink water that has not been boiled, and to do a great many other pleasant things like these. *You* do them every day, and never think about it at all; but if you lived in China, and wished to keep well, so you could help the people, you would have to be careful all the time about what went into your mouth! Going home in this way is called "taking a furlough."

It was while father and mother and Florence were having this pleasant visit at home that

Sonny came to live with them. Not long after this, they came back to China.

Wai Chow is the name of the Chinese city where Florence and Sonny live. That is, they live just outside. The city has a high wall all around it. There are gates in the wall, and at night these gates are shut and locked. This is to keep out robbers, and also because it is an old, old custom, and the Chinese like to keep on doing the same things that their fathers and grandfathers and "great-greats" did. They do not care much for new ways.

There are two pleasant mission homes in the little "compound" where Florence and Sonny live. When the missionaries in China go to a city or a town to work, they buy a piece of land, and build a wall or a fence around it. On the land they build houses to live in. Sometimes there is a school building too, and sometimes a place where sick people come to get well. Such a group of buildings is called a compound.

Florence and Sonny love their pleasant home. Often and often father goes away "i-tin-er-a-ting." He takes his bed, and mosquito net, and clean clothes, and enough food to last perhaps for a month, and goes away up the river, over the

Really Trulies

mountains, down another river, and so on. He does not go because he likes traveling in this way, or to see the country. He goes to visit the people who have given their hearts to Jesus, and to talk with them, and pray with them, and encourage them to keep on serving the Lord. Such a trip is called "i-tin-er-a-ting."

As often as father went, mother would stay at home with Florence and Sonny, and teach them their lessons, and keep the house, and visit the Chinese homes, and urge the mothers to send their girls to the mission school. She was busy every minute. Every night they all thought of father, and wondered where he was staying, and what he was doing, and if he had something clean and warm to eat.

One day when father had been in China nine years, he said: "I must soon go and visit the chapels again."

"I am going with you," said mother.

"But how can you go? What would we do with the children?" asked father.

"We will take them along," said mother.

"Oh, I'm afraid we couldn't. They might get sick; it would be very hard for you — no good place to wash their clothes, or to cook, or

anything," said father. But mother saw, by the way he said it, how much he really wanted her to go!

"I have thought it all over," she said, "and I am sure, though it will not be easy, that we can manage."

Florence and Sonny were eager to go. They had never been, and they thought it would be great fun.

The first thing to do was to get ready. Mother made many extra loaves of bread, sliced them, and dried the slices in the oven till they were a pretty light-brown color. These she put into tin boxes, and wrapped the boxes in oiled paper, so the toasted bread would keep fresh and good for a long time.

The children's clothes, and the books in which Florence studied her lessons had to go, of course. There were a few small toys, too. Then there were the folding cots, and the bedding, and the mosquito nets, which had to be hung over the beds each night to keep away the mosquitoes. Sometimes there were so many mosquitoes, even in the daytime, that mother and Florence and Sonny had to get onto a bed, under the net, to avoid their sharp stings!

Besides, there had to be a few dishes to eat from, and overshoes, umbrellas, coats, and so on. All these things were packed, and wrapped up, and tied up into the smallest possible bundles, and carried by Chinese coolies when the journey was by land. When they went by a boat, all their bundles and boxes were piled in one place where they could be watched. These poor people do not know the commandment, "Thou shalt not steal." They only know that they will be punished if they are found out, but that very often they are not caught. So there is a great deal of stealing in China. The missionaries have to watch their things very carefully. But they do this cheerfully, because they wish to teach the people a better way.

One Friday morning, very early, everything was ready. Florence and Sonny were running up and down the steps, eager to start. Father was counting the bundles and making a list of them; mother was busy doing all the "last things"; and the coolies were doing a great deal of talking, as they always do. Two sedan chairs, with their bearers, were waiting in the yard.

It was a pleasant morning. All of the way father walked, and the children sat together in

his chair, going up and down, up and down, with every step of the bearers, as the men who carry the chairs are called. If the chair coolies are tired, and wish to have you get out and walk, they can make it uncomfortable by jouncing the chair till you feel seasick; but if they are careful, this way of traveling is not unpleasant for a little while, though it gets tiresome after a time.

At noon they came to the first chapel. A Chinese chapel does not look like a little church at home. It is a room or a number of rooms in a group of Chinese buildings. Nearly all these chapels that Florence and Sonny visited have schools for Chinese boys and girls.

Sometimes there are only a few of these Chinese school children, ten or twenty or thirty; but some of the schools have as many as seventy-five. They all study "out loud," and that means *very* loud, most of the time, so there is a great deal of noise in the room. If a visitor comes, they try to make him think they are studying extra hard, by saying their reading lessons over and over as loud as they can.

When the bearers set down the chairs, Florence and Sonny stepped over the long poles by which they were carried, and wondered what they were going to do next.

A room was ready for them, and though it was not very clean, it would do. You do not expect clean rooms where you go i-tin-er-a-ting. That is one reason you go, to show the people how to keep their homes better, and to make them places where good angels will love to stay.

The boxes and bundles were all brought in and counted, the cots were set up, the beds made, and the mosquito nets stretched above them. In one corner was a square Chinese table, and here the dishes were unpacked. There were a few benches and stiff chairs too.

By sunset everything was in "apple pie order" father said, and the people came to the chapel for the evening meeting. That night the children were so tired that they slept as soundly as if they had been in their own snug beds at home. Mother was almost too tired to sleep at all!

When morning came they were all awake early, and each helped made the room tidy while mother cooked rice in the chapel "kitchen." She did not feel very hungry when breakfast was on the table, but Florence and Sonny were ready to eat.

You would think it great fun to see a Chinese

boy and girl come to your Sabbath school, wouldn't you? Maybe you would spend so much time looking at them that the teacher would find it hard to teach the lesson. Well, Chinese boys and girls are just like you; they thought it fun to see two "foreign children," and they looked and looked and *looked*, and pointed shy fingers, and giggled soft little giggles, and clapped their grimy hands over their mouths! Florence and Sonny loved the dear little Chinese children, and soon made friends with them.

This story is long enough. I shall tell you a little more about this i-tin-er-a-ting journey another time.

When Bread Tasted Like Cake

An I-tin-er-a-ting Journey, No. 2

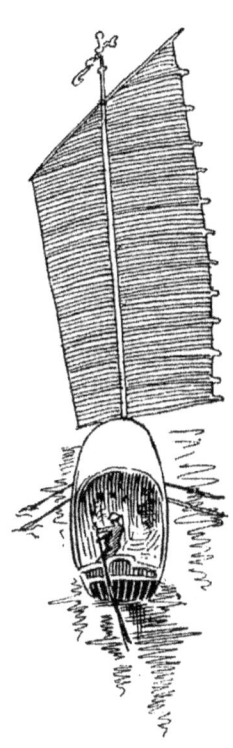

FATHER and mother and Florence and Sonny stayed only over Sabbath at the first chapel where they stopped. On Sunday, father walked off in a pouring rain to visit a village some distance away. When he came back, they packed up their things ready to start off again.

This time they went by boat, walking more than a mile in the rain to the river bank. A little boat was waiting here, and farther out in the river, where the water was deeper, was a steam launch. It was very late when they reached this larger boat, and there was no room on it for them to sleep, or even to lie down on the floor! Every bit of space was full.

Father piled up the bundles, and mother sat on them, holding Sonny on her lap, so he could take a nap. Early in the morning they came to

the next chapel; but it was so small and so dirty, and there were so many flies, that they could not rest.

You know how it is about flies at home. They carry filth on their little hairy legs; and when they crawl about on the food, they leave it there. If we eat such food, we are likely to be ill.

In China, flies are very dirty indeed. But the people do not know it, so they do not try to get rid of them. In the summer time, I have often seen thin slices of watermelon for sale (Chinese boys and girls like watermelon very much) that were so covered with flies that I could not tell which were seeds and which were flies! A great many children are very sick in watermelon time in this land.

One time, Florence and Sonny and father and mother waited twelve hours by a river bank for a boat. When it came, and they were all out on the river, a band of robbers began to shoot at them. But the angels kept them, and they got safely away.

The poor people in the places that Florence and Sonny visited at this time were having a famine. Often they did not have anything at all to eat. You know that in Bible days the peopl used to have famines, and China has them now. Almost all the time there is a famine in some part of this great country.

Many people had so little to eat that they went to the mountains, and dug out the roots of trees, dried them, ground them into a sort of meal, and then made it into porridge. In some places bowls of rice gruel were given out, and the people came by hundreds to get them. Every day starving women and children came to the door, and begged for food. Some of them would walk right in, and snatch the rice out of the kettle in which it was cooking.

Florence and Sonny got hungry, too. "Mother, I have eaten rice for fifteen days, and it just will not *go down*," said Florence one day.

Mother knew how it was. She was very hungry herself. The rice they had was poor and hardly fit to eat.

"I am sorry, dear," she said; "but we have more than fifteen days yet to eat it, so we must be brave and not complain. We are doing it for Jesus, and He will help us."

When father and mother came to towns where there were other missionaries, they called on them. These good men and women were always

Five times angry soldiers shot at the boat.

kind. One time a missionary family invited them to dinner, and gave them some string beans and some tomatoes that they had raised in their own garden. They also gave them a loaf of bread and a pot of jam.

Florence and Sonny thought they had never tasted bread like that! "It tastes like cake," they said.

"Better than cake," said father.

They cut off four thin slices for each meal, to make it last as long as it would, and ate it so *slowly!* Of course there was no butter, but they did not mind *that*.

They were all busy every day. Father taught the people, and mother talked to the women, and told them how to keep well, and how to take care of the babies when they were sick, and many other things. Besides, she cooked the food, helped Florence with her lessons, and heard her recite when she had learned them.

Florence helped too. She washed dishes, and tidied the small room, and helped look after Sonny. Besides this she learned to crochet! So you can see she was busy, and of course she was happy; for busy children are almost always happy children.

One day father and mother started out, with Florence and Sonny, in a drenching rain. There were two sedan chairs for mother and the children, but father walked. They were going to travel forty miles over the mountains.

"Why did they go in the rain?" do you want to know. It was this way. Father had sent word to the people that he was coming, and he knew that no matter if it did rain, they would be waiting for him. So he must not disappoint them. It would have been more pleasant if the sun had been shining, but they must go, anyway.

By and by their chair coolies began to get tired. Sometimes they fell down. Mother and Florence got out and walked, up hill and down. On level places they would get into the chairs, but where the walking was hard, they got out. Mother walked twelve miles that day, and Florence almost as far. Sonny walked some too, but not much; his chubby little legs got tired too easily.

It was almost ten o'clock when they came to the place where they were going to stay that night. They were oh so tired, and *oh* so wet, and OH so hungry! Father set up the beds, and mother made some rice gruel. They all took off their wet clothes and spread them around to

dry. It was very late when they got to bed.

Early the next morning they were off again; for they had twenty-four miles to travel that day. Father's feet were so sore that he had to walk very slowly, so it was late when they came to the chapel, and again very late when they were ready for bed.

One day when they were walking in the rain, they had to wade across many shallow rivers. More than once the water and mud came to their knees. Then father would take Sonny on his back, and carry him across, and set him down on the other side.

My, but they were all wet and dirty! The bedding got wet too, and all the clothes and books and food.

Sometimes when things were very hard, the children would think of the quiet mission compound at Wai Chow, but they did not complain. Not once did the family say they would turn back and go home. They just kept on and on till every chapel had been visited.

But after a while the journey ended, as all journeys do, and the happy day came when they were home again. Never did home look so good before.

"I never knew how nice home is!" said Florence.

"I never want to go away!" said Sonny.

"We must not forget to thank our loving Father for sending His angels with us, and keeping us all the way, and bringing us safely back again," said father.

"I am glad we could go, and sometime we will go again," said mother. "I shall know better what to do, and we must help these poor people all we can."

Sonny's Bible Promise

An I-tin-er-a-ting Journey, No. 3

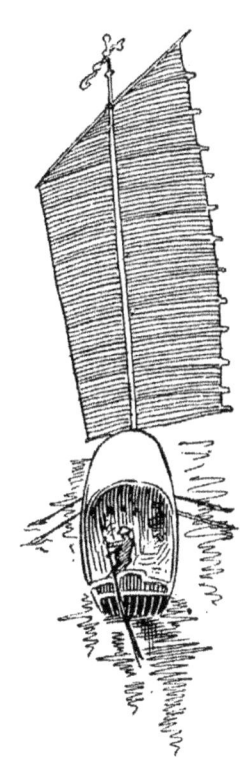

ONE morning father and mother and Florence and Sonny got into a small boat, at ten o'clock with all their bags and bundles. They traveled all day, and about ten o'clock that night they heard men shouting to them from the river bank. Father knew they were robbers.

All along many of the river banks in China are bands of men armed with guns and knives. They steal from the people who travel in boats. These wicked men are called river pirates. Sometimes they are driven away; but more seem to come, and there is always trouble. It is not very pleasant traveling on a river in some parts of China!

Father had met these robbers many times, and had all his things taken by them. So when they told him to stop, he knew what to do. The boat was pulled over to the shore, and a lamp was lighted, and held up so the robbers could see that the people on the boat were foreigners.

Father spoke to them pleasantly, and told them that he was just a *muk-su* (which means pastor) going down the river. He asked them to come to the boat, and by and by some of them came. They looked just like other Chinese men, only they had guns and knives. Some of them wore long silk coats. They asked for "tea money," and father gave them two dollars. In return they gave him their card, and told him there was another band of robbers down the river, but if father would show them this card, they would let him pass.

Often on these journeys father says that the same God who sent His angel to keep the lions from hurting Daniel, sends His angels to soften the hearts of these wicked men. Father believes in the angels, and so do mother and Florence and Sonny.

By and by they came to the other band, but when father told them he had a card, they said, "All right, go on."

The Chinese who love Jesus are glad to have father and mother come to see them, and talk to

them, and tell them how to live. One time an old, old woman, who heard that mother was going to visit a chapel where she came sometimes, walked twenty miles to see her and to be baptized.

One day the box that had all the clean clothes in it, and the books and the medicines, fell into the river! My, that was a sorry time! It was a good thing it was not raining; for by working hard all day they got the things washed and dried and packed up again.

One time after a long trip, the family were in a boat on a river going toward Swatow, a large Chinese city on the sea. Every little while robbers would come to the boat, and yell, and talk, and look at everything. But every time they came, father prayed, and the men went on. These were wild looking men, who did not speak the language that father understands.

In the afternoon one day they sailed around the base of a mountain — and right in front of them were two armies just beginning a battle! On one shore was a little camp of robbers, so father told the boatman to pull over there, and anchor behind a big rock. All the afternoon the boom!

boom! boom! of the big guns roared and echoed through the hills.

There was nothing to do but wait and pray.

Father read the ninety-first Psalm and other comforting promises from the Bible. Once, when the noise was very bad, Sonny repeated his favorite verse, "Let not your heart be troubled."

"If we trust God, we are safe anywhere," he said.

And God took care of them all. In the evening they crossed the river to the other side, where it seemed more quiet. But all night the noise and yelling went on, and no one could sleep.

In the morning it was worse than ever. The army that was losing came over to the side where father's boat was, and began to get ready to fight right there. So father urged his men to row the boat up stream to a more sheltered place.

Here they bought some rice and eggs and vegetables, and had something to eat. Mother had all their money, in silver, in a stocking around her neck, and it was heavy to carry.

They did not know what to do. It might be they would have to leave the boat and everything in it, and flee to the hills.

By and by they saw soldiers on the

Really Trulies 49

other side of the river, running up stream as fast as they could go. They were going so fast that they were almost hidden by dust.

The shooting stopped. All was quiet. So father urged the boatmen to go on down the river. He thought they would see the other army when they came to the city not far away. But when they came, there were no soldiers! They had run away, too! They had run down the river, and their enemies had run up the river. So the way was open for father and mother and the children to go on toward Swatow. "This is the Lord's doing," father said.

Their troubles were not all over, though. Many soldiers wanted the boat they were in, and sometimes they took it, and made the boatmen carry them for a distance. Five times angry soldiers shot at the boat. Father made a little fort out of the charcoal with which it was loaded, and they sat down behind that when the soldiers were shooting.

Three days father and mother and the children spent on the river, this time, to travel ninety miles, and in all this region there was war. But they reached Swatow safely, and from there went gladly home again. The Lord kept them all the way.

4—R. T.

A Flower Story

It was a pleasant May day,
   Oh very long ago!
The sky all white and blue above,
   The earth all green below,
When two small maids with spelling-books
   Went tripping home from school —
A school where easy tasks were set,
   And kindness was the rule!

Two little maids with spelling-books,
   And as they homeward walked,
They stopped to pick the dandelions,
   And happily they talked;
Till all at once both little maids
   The selfsame moment spied
The very king of dandelions
   In all the countryside.

He was a haughty dandelion,
   And straight and very tall,

He stood among the golden hosts,
   His head above them all.
"*It's mine!* IT'S MINE!" cried Minniebelle
   As on both quickly ran.
"I saw it first, you selfish thing!
   Now — get it if you can!"

As Phyllis snatched the flower away,
   Belle's tears began to flow.
'Tis queer what very little things
   Will make a quarrel grow.
Why, all about these tearful maids,
   A-shining in the grass,
Ten thousand cheerful dandelions
   Laughed gay to see them pass.

And when, victorious, in her hand
   Our Phyllis held the prize,
Its gold of shining color
   Grew tarnished in her eyes;
And before her clear-eyed mother
   Possession brought a sting
That made the gay king dandelion
   A very hateful thing.

Alice May hands the book to Mrs. Rose and is invited in.

The Cornucopia

"I WISH I could send this book over to Mrs. Rose," said Mrs. Lewis.

"Oh mamma, let me take it! I know the way," said Alice May. She was six years old.

"All right, you may go," said mother, after a moment. "You may stay a little while if you like, but — don't forget."

You see, Alice May had a habit that some other little girls have had, before and since. When she saw anything she liked, she would ask, or almost-ask, for it. But in those days, well-bred little girls, even if they lived in very small houses in tiny villages, did not ask for things that were not offered to them, when they went to call. "You can always be polite, even if you are poor," they were told.

Alice May knew well what mother meant when she said, "Don't forget."

"Yes, mother," she said.

"And thank Mrs. Rose for the book," added mother, as she tied the strings of Alice May's best ruffled pink sunbonnet under her chin. All this happened long ago. Many little girls wore sunbonnets, and liked them, in those days.

Down the road skipped Alice May, over the bridge, and around the corner; and there was Mrs. Rose's house, all white and green behind its neat picket fence.

Feeling ever so grown-up, Alice May wiped her shoes on the braided door-mat, and pulled the shining bell. There was no bell at Alice May's house. You rapped instead.

"Why, if it isn't Alice May!" said Mrs. Rose. "Come right into the parlor, and wait a minute till I get a pie ready for the oven. Look at the pictures in the album, if you like, or at anything else," she added, as she rushed away.

Alice May was very happy. She looked at the pictures in the album and on the walls. She was not a meddlesome little girl, but she felt softly of the frosty white curtains, and admired the delicate fern-leaf pattern. If she ever had lace curtains, they should have a fern-leaf pattern, she thought. There were other things she liked to look at, too, but the thing she liked best of all

Really Trulies 55

was a little "cornucopia" made in the shape of an ice cream cone and worked with green zephyr. It was pinned high up on one of the frosty lace curtains.

She mustn't ask for it, and she mustn't hint. Still — she couldn't seem to help looking at it, and when Mrs. Rose came back, she began to talk about it.

"That is a very pretty cornucopia," she said, primly.

Mrs. Rose's brown eyes smiled, and she looked at Alice May pleasantly. She understood very well the wish that lay behind the words.

"Do you like it, child? Then you shall have it for your own," she said.

And in half a minute Alice May had the cornucopia in her hands, and was saying, "Oh, *thank* you!" instead of, "*No*, thank you."

Very soon after that she was on her way home, — around the corner, over the bridge, and up the street.

Some way she was not quite happy. What would mother say? Mother would not be pleased: Alice May was not pleased, herself.

But she was an honest little girl, so she walked

out to the side porch where mother was shelling peas, and showed her the cornucopia.

"Why, where did you get that, dear?"

"Mrs. Rose gave it to me."

"Did you ask for it?" Mother looked serious.

"No, mother — not — really."

"Tell me just what you did say, Alice."

"I said, 'That is a very pretty cornucopia, Mrs. Rose,'— and it *is* pretty, mother."

"So it is; but Mrs. Rose would not have thought of giving it to you this morning if she had not seen, from your speaking of it and looking at it so longingly, that you wanted it. You didn't mean to hint, but sometimes it's better not to say anything, for hinting is really worse than asking right out. Now the thing to decide is, are you going to grow up always wanting things that do not belong to you? If you are, there will come a time when even kind persons, like Mrs. Rose, will dread to see you coming. Or are you going to be happy and contented with what you have, even if it is not just like what someone else has? If you are, and always think about what you can do for others instead of what they will do for you, everyone will love you and be glad to see you. Now get your little pan, dear, and help me finish these peas. It's so shady and cool on the porch."

Alice May loved to help. Shelling peas is pleasant work, and soon the heaped-up basket was nearly empty. By and by —

"Mother, what shall I do about the — the — cornucopia?" she asked.

"What do *you* think?"

"I — I — think I'd better take it back," said Alice May.

"That is a good idea," said mother. "You may go this afternoon when it begins to get cool." She kissed the top of the little pink sunbonnet when the time came, and watched Alice May going slowly down the walk.

> Oh, but it was hard to go!
> Though she walked as slow as slow,
> Bravely trying not to cry,
> Still her footsteps seemed to fly.
>
> > Like a dreadful waking dream
> > Past the houses, past the stream,
> > Round the corner, down the street,
> > Sped, so swift, her lagging feet!
>
> Here's the house, and in she goes;
> There's no other way, she knows.

> Firmly, then, I'm glad to tell,
> Alice pulled the shining bell.

"Back again!" cried Mrs. Rose. "But what is the matter, dear child?" For she saw the tears that Alice May was winking back as hard as she could.

"I — I — hinted for this,— and so — I've brought it back," asid Alice May, slowly. "I'm sorry."

"I see," said Mrs. Rose, who really did see. She took the cornucopia, laid it up on a shelf, and began to talk about something else just as if nothing had happened. That gave Alice May a chance to get over her tears. And Mrs. Rose smiled so kindly and told her such pleasant stories about the pictures on the wall, that pretty soon she was feeling happy and glad she had come.

"I've a little plan," said Mrs. Rose, when it was time for Alice May to go; "I have some pieces of cardboard, and some pink and blue and green zephyrs. If you and Clara Van Wormer will come over Thursday afternoon, I'll show you how to make ever so many pretty things. Would you like that?"

This was the time to say, "O, *thank* you!" And Alice May said it with shining eyes, then home she ran as fast as she could, to tell mother.

"That will be fine," said mother.

"I'm so glad I took it back," said Alice May.

"I'm glad about ever so many things," said mother, smiling.

Be True, Be Kind

BE true, little laddie, be true,
From your cap to the sole of your shoe!
O, we love a lad with an honest eye,
Who scorns deceit and who hates a lie;
Whose spirit is brave, and whose heart is pure,
Whose smile is open, whose promise sure;
Who makes his mother a friend so near
He'll listen to nothing she may not hear;
Who's his father's pride and his sister's joy —
A hearty, thorough, and manly boy;
Who loves on the playground a bat and ball,
But will leave fun bravely at duty's call;
Who's as pleasant at work as he is at play,
And takes a step upward with each new day.
    Then be true, little laddie, be true!

Be kind, little maiden, be kind!
On life's busy way you will find
There is always room for a girl who smiles,

And with loving service the hour beguiles;
A lass who is thoughtful as she is fair,
And for others' wishes has a care;
Who is quick to see when the heart is sad,
And is loving and tender to make it glad;
Who loves her mother, and lightens her cares,
And many a household duty shares;
Who is kind to the aged and kind to the young,
And laughing, and merry, and full of fun.
There is always love for a girl who is sweet,
Always a smile her smile to greet.
 Then be kind, little maiden, be kind!

True and his mother were happy when they returned home with their arms full of bundles.

True's Money

And What He Bought With It

THE summer that he was ten years old, True earned ten dollars. That was a long time ago, when little boys did not have many ways to earn money. They did not get paid for bringing in the wood, or feeding the chickens, or picking up chips. True did harder work than this, too, but he never thought of taking money from father and mother for the things he did to help them.

You would have liked True, I know, he had such dark, merry eyes, and such dark, curly hair, and his cheeks were so red, and his teeth were so white, and his mouth was so smiling. He liked to play, too; but he was a chubby little boy, and could not run so fast as his brother. But he could wrestle, and no boy of his own size could throw him down.

True's father and mother were very poor.

They lived on a farm that was not all cleared yet so corn and wheat and oats could grow on it. Every year they all worked hard to get it ready for crops, but there was never much to sell. They had corn to be ground into meal for pancakes and porridge, and sometimes wheat for white bread. When there was a cow, they had good milk. For a long time they did not have any fruit; but as soon as he could, father set out young apple trees. By and by these small trees grew larger, and began to bear apples enough for all the family, and after a while there were some for the neighbors who did not have any of their own. But that took a long time.

True had four sisters and one brother. You can see that with so many to feed, and so little to sell, there was not much money in that house from one year to another.

When he was ten years old, True began to wish that he could get pretty things for his sisters such as other little girls had. There was Jennie, who went to the same district school. She had a plaid dress. True thought it the prettiest dress he had ever seen in his life; and it was a pretty dress and a pretty and sweet little girl who wore it.

Really Trulies 65

Of course there were boys in the school who had good clothes, too; but True never thought about wishing he could get such clothes for himself! But he did think and think and *think* how he could get a pretty dress for each of his sisters. By and by he thought of a plan.

"If I work fast, and get all my weeding done early, may I go and pick berries?" he asked his father one day.

"If you do it well, you may," said father.

True worked quickly, and soon the last row was clean. Then he started to the berry patch in the edge of the woods to pick berries. He didn't like to pick berries very well, but he hoped he could sell them in the village, and he could not think of any other way to earn money.

So he picked as fast as he could, and by and by he had two wooden pails full. The empty pails were very heavy for a little boy to carry; and when they were filled with berries, they were heavier still.

But he lugged one a little way, and then the other a little way, and finally was home with them. Now they must be taken a mile and a half to town. It was late in the afternoon, and a hard walk even without such a load. But True had

made up his mind to work hard, and he did not care.

When he came home that night, he was oh so tired, but happy, for he had two dollars in his pockets, almost the first money he had ever earned.

Besides, one or two women had asked him to bring berries to them to-morrow.

The next day he picked again, and the next and the next and the next. He was tired before the week was over. One day some larger boys, to tease him, picked up dirt from the road and threw it over the tops of the pails of berries. Poor little True!

But he kept right on, and by the time there were no more berries to pick, he had ten dollars. He did not know about giving back to the Lord one tenth of all the money that He helps us to earn, or I am sure he would have counted out one dollar from his little store the very first thing.

Now what secrets mother and True had to talk about! for he told her what he was planning to do — that is, all but *one* thing. There must be a dress for Sue and one for Anna and one for Mary, and a doll for Debbie Dear, and a shirt and necktie for father, and a cap for Brother Will.

They could not get plaid dresses, they knew. Even in those days, when cloth cost so much less than now, there was not enough money for plaid like Jennie's school dress. But gingham was next best, and would do very well. Over and over, True set down on his slate just what the money would buy.

1 caP, Will	$1.00
1 sHirt, father	.50
1 Tie, father	.50
1 G. dres, Sue	1.50
1 same, Anna	1.50
1 more dres, Mary	1.00
1 Dol, Debbie Deer	1.00
	$7.00

You see, True could not spell very well yet, but he could add all right.

That left three dollars. "What are you going to buy for yourself, Trueboy?" asked mother. She did not think, you see, any more of asking what True was going to buy for *her*, than True thought of buying anything for himself!

At last the happy day came when True and mother went to town to buy the things.

Sometimes the road had seemed long to True, but to-day it seemed short. He felt as if he was hardly walking at all, he was so happy.

And what fun it was to look at the ginghams, and decide just which was prettiest, and which would look nicest on Sue and Anna and Mary! There was a little money left over when everything was bought, even to the prettiest doll that True had ever seen. A little extra, I mean, besides the three dollars that True had not told his mother about spending. With these extra dimes and pennies True bought small hard candies that would last a long time, and a whole quart of peanuts!

"And now what are we going to do?" asked mother, when, their arms full of bundles, they came out of the store.

"Come with me, and I'll show you," said True.

"Oh, *no*, Trueboy!" said mother, when she saw that True was taking her to the store where women's shoes were sold.

But when his happy look changed to grief, she went in with him, and he bought her a pair of new shoes, and rubbers besides! In those days you really could buy a pair of good shoes for two dollars and a half, and a pair of rubber overshoes for fifty cents!

"But you have nothing for yourself," said mother.

"All these things are for me, mother," he said; "when you have them, it is just the same as if I had them all!"

And though every one at True's house was happy that day, I know that True was really the happiest of them all. He had the "more blessed" kind of happiness, the kind that comes from giving and not from receiving.

Father and Mother went every evening to the tent, and took the children.

Picking Up Grubs

WHEN True was twelve years old, a man came to the village near the farm where he lived, and told the people about the Sabbath, and the soon coming of Jesus, and other things that they had never heard before.

Father and mother went every evening to the tent, and took the children. Before the meetings were ended, they decided that they would serve the Lord, keep His holy Sabbath, and live to please Him day by day. True gave his heart to Jesus too.

They were still working on the farm, trying to get the trees all cut down, which seems a pity when one thinks how beautiful they were, and how long they had been growing there. But you cannot have curly maple trees and wheat growing in the same field. Besides, children can't eat trees, and they can eat bread — so there you are! And there were six children in True's home, you remember.

First, the trees were chopped down. Then father rolled them into great piles, and set fire to them, and burned them. One hates to think of all that lovely wood being burned in that way, but it was,— not even in a stove to keep people warm, but out in the open field.

The beautiful woods were a sorry looking place when the big timber was cut, and the ground had all been burned over. Then the stumps had to be dug and pulled out of the ground one by one. That was hard work. And the roots had to be grubbed out with a grub-hook. Hard, back-breaking work, day after day. It seemed sometimes as if it would never all be done!

It was True's work to pick up grubs, as the roots which were dug up were called. There were hundreds and thousands of them, scraggly, scratchy things, covered with earth, some of them almost too heavy to move.

True hated the grubs and hated the work.

The more he thought about it, the more he disliked picking up grubs, and piling them to burn. They tore his bare hands, and the briers scratched his bare feet. No little boy, it seemed to him, ever had so hard a time as he.

But there the grubs were, in the south field,

and they had to be picked up. It was father's plan to get the field cleared that year. And it was True's job to pick up the grubs.

One day he was working all alone, and feeling very cross about it, too. He was hot and pricky and thirsty, and no matter how hard he worked, there seemed to be just as many grubs the next day as there were the day before.

"I believe they grow in the night," he said to himself. And he sat down on a stump to rest and feel sorry for himself.

While he was sitting there, a little Thought came into his head. I think the good angel who was with True all those days sent it.

"You can like your work if you try," was the Thought.

True said it over to himself. "I can like my work if I try!" Why, he had never thought of that before! He could like, if he tried, picking up grubs, and going after the cows when it was rainy and dark, and weeding the garden, and picking potato bugs,— and turning the grindstone!

"I'll *try* it!" said True.

And he *did* try it, and kept right on trying. "I like to pick up grubs," he said over and over,

and whistled and sang as he worked there all alone, piling them up. Someway he seemed to make a bigger pile, that way, too. And by and by, not that day nor the next, but after a really hard summer, the grubs were all cleared out of the south field, and every day was a happy day for True while he worked.

True remembered that little Thought all his life, and worked on that plan. As he grew older, he had many hard things to do, many things that he would not have enjoyed at all, if he had not remembered that you can like your work, no matter how hard, if it is yours to do and must be done. You can like it if you *try*!

And if you like your work, you are happy while you are doing it. That is why True was a happy little boy, and a happy bigger boy, and a happy young man, and a happy older man,— happy all the time.

Neighborhood Nuisance or Neighborhood Joy

WILLIE P. PORTER and Eleanor Dwight
Are heedless and thoughtless from morning till night.
They are noisy in talking and quarrelsome at play,
And are often heard shouting, "Get out of my way!"
They laugh and speak rudely when age passes by,
And count it all fun to make small children cry.
They scatter torn papers about on the street,
And trample the hedges down under their feet;
The flowers that their owners have tended with pride,
They snatch from their gardens, and then toss aside.

The neighbors say, "O that we might have a rest!
Such children are surely a nuisance and pest."

(75)

Tommy T. Harter and Dorothy Mann
Both behave as politely as any one can.
When calling on friends, they are quiet and sweet,
And always wipe off all the mud on their feet.
They rise up at once when their elders appear,
Their voices in speaking are pleasant and clear;
They do not tramp over the gardens and flowers,
Or play hide and seek on the street at late hours;
They are thoughtful of others, and gentle, and
 kind,
And at school all the rules they are careful to mind.
The neighbors are frequently heard to remark,
 "We are glad that these children reside in the
 Park!"

Now which will *you* be, Little Girl, Little Boy,
A Neighborhood Nuisance, or Neighborhood Joy?

The Blue Cloud

Do you wonder what a *blue cloud* is? You know white clouds, of course, the tiny ones so high up in the summer sky, like little balls of snowy cotton; and the long, fine, spreading-out kind called mare's tails, that often come a day or two before a storm; and the fluffy white clouds that look like sheep in a pasture; and the big, heavy, black clouds that bring the rain in summer time.

But — a *blue* cloud!

And there were not only blue clouds, but red ones and green and pink and gray and brown, and ever so many other colors!

A "cloud" of this kind was a long, loosely woven scarf to wear around the neck and over the head. All the little girls had them when Etta May went to Miss Maria King's private school. Big girls and women wore them too. Everybody had to have a "cloud," it seemed, if

she were to be at all comfortable. But why these "clouds" were *called* "clouds," I haven't the least idea.

Etta May's cloud was wine color — a "good color, for it won't show the dirt," said mother.

Dolly Delight was dainty, and always looked neat and clean. Her shoes did not seem to get muddy, her rubbers always looked shiny, her knit cap always sat down so jauntily on her smooth head! Even her gray checked coat, which was as like Etta May's coat as two coats could possibly be, seemed to look better. In the summer she had a blue silk parasol, with ruffles, the prettiest that Etta May had ever seen.

And now,— Dolly Delight Randall's cloud was blue! And blue, pale blue, the soft blue of a summer sky or forget-me-nots in early spring, was the color of all colors that Etta May loved best.

To see Dolly Delight putting on her little gray coat, and setting her jaunty cap on her smooth head, and then wrapping that lovely blue cloud around her neck made Etta May feel naughty deep down inside.

But she didn't talk about it.

She knew very well that mother would be

ashamed of her; she knew, too, that she ought to be ashamed of herself.

Still, she kept thinking about the blue cloud. She wouldn't have minded so much if it had belonged to anyone else, she told herself. But Dolly Delight,—well, she didn't like Dolly Delight, anyway. "Teacher's pet," she called her, and remembered with hot cheeks how Miss Maria King had kept her in at recess for whispering that very morning. Dolly Delight had whispered too, but she did it quietly, and she did not have to stay in at recess.

All these were very bad thoughts to run around in a little girl's head; they ought to have been driven outside the first thing, and the doors shut and locked so they could not come in again. For if you keep bad thoughts in your mind, bad actions are sure to follow.

By and by Etta May went out to the well to get a drink; and when she came in, a class was reciting.

In the hall were all the children's coats and caps and overshoes and clouds. Blue, violet, red, and yellow the clouds were, all the colors of the rainbow. Her own cloud was hanging in its place over her coat. It was the darkest color

there, and Dolly Delight's was the prettiest of all.

Quick as a wink Etta May took hold of the lovely blue cloud, and tore a long rent in it. Then she went quietly into the room, and sat down.

Dolly Delight did not see the tear when she went home, but her mother saw it, and mended it so neatly that no one could have told where it was. She thought it had caught on a nail, and been "snagged." Dolly Delight did not remember tearing it, but she said she would be careful. Dolly Delight was always careful.

The days passed, and the weeks, and the months. Etta May did not tell, but she felt unhappy. By and by the "clouds" were all folded away for next winter, school was out, and the long days of summer play had come.

Whenever Etta May saw Dolly Delight, she was ashamed. Whenever she knelt down to say her prayer at evening, she thought of the way her hands looked when they were tearing the cloud. The rent in the blue cloud came to seem like a black scar on her heart.

"I cannot bear it any longer," she told her mother one evening, and then she sobbed the whole miserable story out with her head on mother's shoulder. It was strange how much better she felt when mother knew.

Then of course she had to tell Dolly Delight. That was very much harder.

"I don't care," said Dolly Delight when Etta May had told her how sorry she was. "I never even knew it anyway. That's all right."

Etta May knew that it was not all right, but that she had done the best she could to make it right. And she made up her mind that as long as she lived she would be just as glad when other people had things that she liked, even things she *wanted*, as if she had them herself.

Plans

"When I'm a man," said little Paul,
"I'm never going to work at all;
I'll never have split wood to pile.
Or cows to fetch for half a mile;
I'll never pull a single weed,
Nor carry milk the calf to feed.
From morning till the set of sun,
I'll play and have all kinds of fun."

Now Paul has grown to be a man,
He's working on another plan.
"I'll work from morn till night each day,
And when I'm old, I'll stop and play!
I'll fetch the cows home half a mile,
And cut the grass, and weed awhile.
I'll be a boy again, care free,
And every hour will happy be."

I'll whisper, Paul, what you must do
If you'd have fun your whole life through:
Enjoy your work, enjoy your play,
And you'll be happy every day.

Milton's Honan Pledge

MILTON lived in America. He was seven years old, "going on eight," when his teacher in church school told her Junior Missionary Volunteer Society about Honan, and showed it to them on a map of China. She told them how large it is, and how many millions of Chinese live there. Honan is a province of China, just as Michigan is a state in the United States, and York is a county in the British Isles.

She told them a little about the children of Honan, and the kind of houses they live in, and what kind of food they eat. Chenchu was a little Honan girl. Her father's house was fairly good. There was a raised platform at one end, made of bricks. This was the bed, and all the family slept on it. There was heat under the bricks, to keep them warm.

The people in Honan who have a warm bed like this are very glad. Many do not have even this much. A great many die of cold and hunger every year in Honan.

Most of the houses there are very poor. Some are so low they do not look like houses at all. They are made by sticking a number of bamboo poles in the ground, bending the tops over, and fastening them together with long, narrow strips of bamboo or with tough dried grass. This framework may be covered with coarse mats, plastered over with mud. All kinds of dried stalks and straw are stacked against the side of the house to keep out the bitter winds. If the family have a pig, it lives right in the house with them, and the chickens go inside, too, at night.

Sometimes the houses are larger, and are made of cakes of yellow-brown mud, which have been dried in the sun. There are many large towns that have only these mud houses, with streets of the same color, and a wall all around of the same mud. They are not pretty places in which to live.

Near an ancient shrine in Honan there is a large and very old cypress tree. Most of the trees in China are cut down for firewood when they are small, but once in a while one is allowed to grow a long time. When a tree is large and old, it is often thought to be sacred. In this cypress tree there is a large hole, and the people believe that by crawling through the hole they will be cured of any sickness which they may have! All the bark has been worn off, and the bare trunk is smooth and shining, where the people have crawled through!

The teacher in the church school wished every one in the Junior Society to make a promise to bring some money before the end of the year, to send to these poor people in Honan to tell them about Jesus.

"I will bring five dollars," said Milton.

"That is a good deal for a little boy," said his teacher; "Are you sure you can? You know this is to be money that you earn yourself, not what mother gives you." Milton was very sure.

"Mother," he said, as soon as he reached home, "the teacher told us all about Honan, and I've promised to give five dollars — going to earn it my own self."

"All right, Milton," said mother. "I am glad you want to help. But you better begin right away to save, for if you promised to give that much, that is a pledge, and a pledge must be kept."

For a little boy, Milton had many ways of earning pennies and nickels and dimes. He took papers to the houses of all the people on a number of streets, he sold magazines, and sometimes he ran errands for people who did not have any little boys of their own. Mrs. Ramsay paid him fifty cents a month for emptying the ashes from her furnace.

Still, his Honan pledge did not grow very fast. You see, there were so many things that he wanted for himself!

Each week the teacher talked a little about the far-off land of China, and about the promises the children had made. Some of them had their money all ready. The end of the year was drawing near. Milton did not like to hear about it.

By and by there was a new thing that Milton wanted, oh, so *much!* A bicycle! You have to be a little boy "going on eight" to know just how much Milton wanted that "wheel." It was shiny, and almost new, and just the right size, and it had such good tires —!

"You see," he explained, "I could get around so much faster with the papers, if I only had it! I've got two dollars now, and I'm going to work

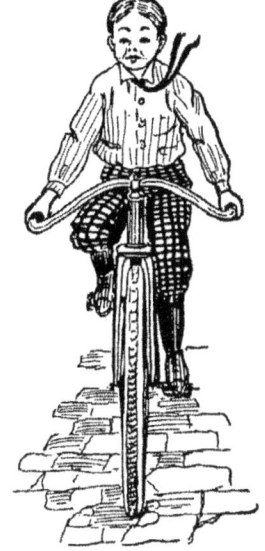

every minute and save all I earn, every penny — can I buy it, mother?"

"But your two dollars is for the Honan pledge, Milton. What about that? And then, you know, you promised to raise five dollars."

Milton did not want to think about anything but the bicycle. That was very near, and Honan a long way off. But he did think about it, just the same, and he thought hard.

"I'm really going to pay that pledge, mother," he said. "I'm not going to buy ice cream cones and peanuts every time I want them. I said I would pay it, and I will."

Of course when he really made up his mind, he really did save the money. It was hard work at first, but the more he saved, the better he liked it; and there was no happier boy in the church school than Milton when he paid his Honan pledge.

And after that, Milton kept on working and saving, till he had enough to buy the bicycle. It took a long time, but he had learned how to save, and that helped. And of course he had great fun on the wheel, as any little boy would; but someway it never gave him so much real "inside happiness" as paying his Honan pledge.

They had the lovely outdoors for a playground.

A Bear Story

HATTIE and Lucy and Willy lived on a small farm among the hills, ever and ever so long ago. They were very poor, but happy just the same, for they had the lovely outdoors for a playground, and in the house the kindest little mother in the world. They thought so, and I think so, too; for when she was an old, old, old lady, I knew her well and loved her much.

The children might play any day in the orchard; and you know how easy big old apple trees are to climb, and what lovely lunches grow right ready to your hand,—"pound sweetings," all yellow as honey and juicy-sweet; "snow apples," crimson outside and white as a glistening snowdrift inside, and oh, so good tasting! "spies," and "strawberries," and many others. No child is really poor who has all the lovely things that children have every day who live on farms in the country.

And the big meadow across the road! Father didn't like the daisies that whitened it every summer, but the children loved them. And through the meadow a little brook ran away on dancing feet to find the river that flowed in and out, in and out, among the green hills.

Usually the children were not allowed to cross the twisting rail fence that separated the south end of the meadow from the "clearing" that lay beyond and reached up to the low hills that grew higher and higher till they formed a range of mountains. There were bears in the woods, and other wild animals, and sometimes they came roaming where they were not wanted.

But now it was berry time; and the children longed to fill their mouths and their pails with the dark, shining fruit. There were never such blackberries as grew on those hills. I know, because a long time after all this happened, I often picked berries there myself.

"Mother, may we go berrying?" asked Hattie. She was the oldest, and the one who usually asked. "We will stay just in the edge of the clearing, and be careful not to get lost or anything."

"Please, mother," said brown-eyed Lucy;

"I'm sure we can find berries enough for supper, and maybe some for jam besides."

"Please! please! please!" piped Willy.

"And what would you do if a bear should chase you, Willyboy?" asked mother, smiling. She smiled, because Willy was so plump and so little that from morning till night he was falling down as often as he tried to run anywhere.

"I'd *run*," said Willy; and they all laughed at that.

"We'll take the best care of him," said Hattie, and mother, after a glance across the road, at the daisy-dotted meadow, and to the clearing beyond, said "Yes." They would hardly be out of her sight, and the berries would be good for supper. She wished that she might slip away from the kitchen and go too.

Away the children ran. Zip, the small, black, curly dog was dashing around the children, or running off on some little sidetrip and back again, as excited as the children themselves.

Through the meadow, across the brook, over the fence,— and there they were! The clearing was full of tangled berry vines, their long arms bending under their load of fruit. What fun it was to hear the first berries tumbling into the

shining pails! In a few minutes they were so full that they would not hold another berry, and three little stomachs were almost as full!

There were flowers in the clearing, and wintergreens, though the spicy leaves were no longer as tender and sweet as they had been a few weeks earlier. There were wild flowers, and ferns, and beds of the softest, greenest moss! It was a lovely place to play.

"We'll stay just a little while," said Hattie, setting the pails of berries carefully in a shady place under a bush, covering them with a few green leaves, and hanging her sunbonnet on the bush so they would not lose sight of it. Then the children played that they were discoverers in a new world, and each one tried to see what he could find that was new and different. It was great fun. Zip dashed here and there, trying to be everywhere at once, as little dogs will when they are happy.

"We'd better go home, now," said Hattie, by and by. "Mother might worry if we stayed any longer."

So they started for the bush where they had left their pails of berries. Zip dashed ahead, but almost at once he dashed back again, barking and yipping at the top of his voice. There was a munching, crunching, rattling sound under the bush — and look! What was that queer, black shape?

"Bear!" cried Willy.

The girls said nothing at all; but quick as quick each took one of Willy's fat little hands, and the three just *flew* through the clearing toward the rail fence.

The bear had finished the berries by this time, and he began to come toward the children with his queer, lumbering walk; but Zip was like a big, black hornet, in front of Bruin, behind him, nipping his legs, dashing up in front of his nose — there was no getting rid of him. Zip was being very brave; for he did not like the bear at all. He could not drive him off, but he could keep him busy while the children ran, and this he did just as well as if he had been much bigger and stronger.

It may be that Bruin would not have hurt the children anyway. Maybe he was only looking around to find where the blackberries grew most thickly. But you do not stop to think of that when a bear is coming after you! No, indeed!

And that big, black bear kept right on after the children. How they did run! It seemed as if they never would get to that fence, and over it! Then they thought: But bears can climb, too! How scared they were. They tried to run faster still, and not once did they stop to look back.

Finally they scrambled over the fence, picked themselves up, and dashed, breathless and panting, across the brook, through the meadow, and into their own safe yard.

"Oh, mother!" they cried, in one breathless breath.

"What is the matter, children?" called mother anxiously, as she hurried to the door.

"Bear!" burst out Willy.

But the children were too much out of breath to say very much for a minute. But soon they began all talking at the same time, they were so excited.

"Oh, I'm so glad we are home again," said Hattie with a long, long sigh when the story was finished.

"So am I, dear children," said mother, as she threw her arms around them all.

At Grandma's

OUR grandma's is the nicest place
   For little girls to play!
When we go there, it always seems
   The time's too short we stay.

The apple trees around the house
   Are pink and white in spring;
Sometimes we catch a fragrant spray
   As back and forth we swing.

Beneath their wide and friendly shade
   We set our tea things out,
I visit Jane, Jane visits me,
   And thus we turn about.

On baking days we have such fun
   With dough and rolling-pin.
Whatever grandma makes we make —
   Pies, cakes, and cookies thin.

At Christmas time, at cherry time,
   And on Thanksgiving too —
If it were not for grandma's house,
   We'd not know what to do!

We're sorry when we say good-by,
   We love dear grandma so;
But "best of friends must part," she smiles,
   To cheer us as we go.

"Now come again, my dears," she says,
   "I'll miss you every day."
Our grandma's is the *nicest* place
   For little girls to play!

Fenton's Fall

FENTON is a dear little boy who lives in China. When he was very small indeed, he came across the wide, blue, Pacific Ocean, with his father and his mother, to live in Shanghai. He is only five years old now — just your age, maybe.

There is one thing about Fenton that is different from most little boys five years old, whom I have seen. He is always friendly, and always pleasant and polite. His voice, when he says "good morning," is just the kind of voice you like to hear. Perhaps that is because he has always heard pleasant voices in his home. Pleasantness is like that, you know; it is "catching," as we say of whooping cough and measles. Wouldn't it be a lovely world to live in if every one was pleasant all the time? Of course it will be that way sometime, and every little boy and girl can help to make one little corner of it that way now. But he is a really truly boy just the same, and likes to climb on the fence, and swing on the gate, and run races with other little boys, and play with his wagon.

When Fenton first came to China, he went with his father and mother to Nanking, where there is a school for missionaries.

"Why!" you say, "Missionaries are grown up. *They* don't need to go to school!"

Yes, they are grown up, but they do need to go to school. They go to learn to speak the queer-sounding Chinese language, and to read the beautiful Chinese writing. The Chinese do not have A B C, as we do, but signs that stand for words or parts of words. It does not look beautiful, at first, to one who has never studied it; but after a time, when one begins to learn, he sees that every character is like a picture. Chinese writing is really a kind of picture writing.

Fenton's father came to China to help make papers and books for the Chinese fathers and mothers and children, but first he had to study very hard. This was the reason he went to Nanking.

When he was ready to begin to make books and papers, he came to Shanghai where the printing

office is. And of course Fenton came with him.

A pleasant mission home was all ready for the family to live in. Some of the mission homes are for two families, one living upstairs and one downstairs, and Fenton's house is that kind. It is a very pleasant upstairs, for you can look out of the window and see, right over the wall, what is passing in the street, and you can see a few green fields, and little clusters of Chinese houses, each group called a village.

There is an attic in this house, with a window in each end. From the window that faces south, you can see ocean ships and river boats sailing slowly up the Whangpoo River; and often you can see the great sails of the Chinese junks, or sailing boats, so stately and tall, going up or down the stream. In many places the big cotton mills shut out this pleasant sight, but there are still a few open spaces where it can be seen.

Ever since he was a tiny boy, father and mother had said to Fenton, when he went near a window, "Fenton, dear, be careful!" "Fenton, *don't* lean out!" "Fenton, you will *surely* fall!" "Watch what you're about!" But some way Fenton didn't hear! When there was anything outside that he wished to see, he would dash up

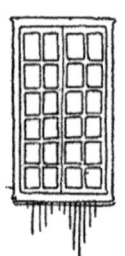

to the window and lean out, if it was open, or press hard against the glass, if it was closed. If there was a screen in the window, he leaned on that. He just couldn't seem to stand by the window and look out.

So until Fenton should really *hear* these warnings, father and mother had to be watching him all the time, and they had to be careful to see that the screens were hooked.

The attic windows are high up from the ground — thirty feet. Just above the windows on the second floor run three strong wires, that bring the electric current into the house to make the bright lights at night.

One day Fenton went up to the attic alone. Father and mother were downstairs. It was Friday afternoon, and they were getting ready for Sabbath. In the next yard Fenton heard the little girls, Helen and Hazel, laughing and playing. Quickly he ran to the window, climbed up on a low box to see better, and leaned all his chubby weight against the screen.

The screen had been closed, but not fastened. Much quicker than it takes to tell it, poor little Fenton was on the ground, thirty feet below.

He had struck on the wires, and bounded off like a rubber ball.

Fenton was very much frigntened, you may well believe; and so were all the neighbors. The father of Helen and Hazel heard the *plump!* that roly-poly Fenton made when he struck the ground, and he was over the fence at once. Father came running down, and the doctor came in his big automobile to feel of the little boy's bones and see if any had been broken.

But the wonderful part of it is that he was not hurt at all. There was the tiniest scratch on the back of his neck, and a little dent above his nose, but the skin was not broken anywhere, and his bones weren't even cracked! He was scared of course, and his poor mother, who was ill, was very badly frightened; but Fenton was all right. Next morning he was in Sabbath school with the rest of the children, smiling and happy.

But since that time Fenton remembers about windows. He does not have to be told not to lean out, and not to lean against the screen. He *knows*.

Can You Tell?

Scowler and Howler are two little boys,
    And Whiner's their sister queer;
The place where they live? O, it's not very far;
    In fact, it is rather near here.

Scowler is touchy and grumpy and cross,
    And often for hours he won't talk;
You never can tell when a "spell" will come on,
    At home, or when taking a walk.

Howler has tumbles and scratches and bumps
    Every hour, it would seem, of the day;
The neighbors are weary of hearing him yell,
    But they live there, and can't move away.

And Whiner, so dainty, so pretty, so fair,
    Is complaining from morning till night;
If she keeps on for long in the way she's begun,
    I'm afraid she will look like a fright!

Now what shall be done for these little folks three?
    And how shall their ways be endured?
Shall we kiss them and coax them from morning till night,
    Or spank them until they are cured?

Modesta's Bible

MODESTA is a little Filipino girl. Her home is on the island of Luzon, the largest of the Philippine Islands, far away in the Pacific Ocean. It is summer all the time in the Philippines. The little brown-skinned boys and girls who live there never go coasting or skating. There is no snow nor ice. Instead of cold weather and hot weather, such as we have, they have hot weather and hotter weather, with a long rainy season. Sometimes so much water falls that even in Manila, the chief city, the water covers many of the streets!

Instead of apples and peaches and pears, the children of the Philippines have papayas and mangoes and cocoanuts. Papayas are something like cantaloupes, only instead of growing on vines on the ground they grow on slender trees close to the top of the trunk.

Mangoes are really delicious when they are ripe. They taste like so many things to so many people that it is not safe to say just what they *do* taste like when fresh; but when they are canned, they taste a little like peaches. They have just one seed, but that one is so large that you are very glad there is only one! It is hard to eat a mango without soiling your fingers, but it can be done, if you are careful, and go slowly. The mango tree is very tall, with wide-spreading limbs and dark-green leaves. It is one of the prettiest trees that grows anywhere.

Cocoanuts you know about, of course. They grow in a cluster near the top of a tall palm. Travelers in the Philippines like to take a green cocoanut, cut a little hole in the top, and drink the cool milk. It is pure and sweet, and is very refreshing when one is thirsty.

The shell of the cocoanut is so firm and hard and tough that these nuts can be sent far over the ocean in ships. They keep fresh and sweet a long time; but mangoes and papayas must be eaten as soon as they are ripe.

Modesta and her father and mother live in a house that is made of bamboo and the leaves of a palm called the nipa palm. It is built up on poles so high that a man can walk under it. This is to keep the floor dry in the rainy season. To get into this house they climb a short ladder of bamboo. If they wish, they can pull the ladder up after them.

The floor is of split bamboo, tied together with narrow strips of rattan. Such a floor is not hard to keep clean, for all the dirt falls down between the cracks!

Modesta loves Jesus. On Sabbaths when she goes to Sabbath school, she knows her lessons well. She always learns the memory verse, and can tell the book and chapter and the number of the verse.

When Modesta was eight years old, her Sabbath school teacher said, "I wonder how many children will try to learn every memory verse this year?" Modesta said she would try. Others said the same thing, but after a few weeks, many of them stopped trying.

Modesta kept right on. Over and over and over she repeated her verses,— ten of them, with book and chapter and verse; twenty, thirty, forty, forty-five, *forty-eight!* It took a long time to repeat them over and over, and at first it was hard not to forget and make mistakes; but she

kept trying till she knew the whole forty-eight, and could say them perfectly.

A large meeting is held once every year in Northern Luzon, something like a campmeeting in America. At that time, all who can do so come to the town where the meeting is held to study the Bible, and to sing and pray.

Modesta's father and mother and all the children came this year. Other families came from other Sabbath schools. Altogether there were seven who had learned all the memory verses for the whole year! On Sabbath, when the little meetinghouse built of bamboo and palm leaves was full of people, Modesta, because she was the youngest of all who had learned the memory verses, was asked to stand up and recite them one by one.

It is easier, you know, to recite them at home, with mother to prompt you at the hard places. But Modesta was not afraid. She knew them all, and she said them straight through, from beginning to end, and told all the books and all the chapters and all the verses too.

The pastor was pleased, and so was every one else who heard; for when a child learns the words of God's Holy Book when he is young, he will not forget them. They will come to his mind when he is sad, or is tempted to do wrong. The Psalmist said, "Thy word have I hid in my heart, that I might not sin against Thee."

Modesta's eyes were shining, and her dark cheeks were pink, when she was through. Then the pastor handed her a little package. It was a pretty, new Bible, all her own! The others who had learned the verses had Bibles just like hers, but no one there was more happy that day than Modesta. I hope that she will keep on year after year learning her verses, and saying them over, and thinking about what they mean. If she does this, they will be just what the Bible says, a lamp to her feet, and a light to her path.

(108)   *Friends again, "Good bye."*

The Locket

MISS MARIA KING'S SCHOOL for Little Girls was held in the "parlor" of a big, old-fashioned house in the village where Laura Louise lived. There were low tables for the Little Girls, and small chairs to sit on. In one corner of the room was a whatnot filled with shells that Miss Maria's sailor brother had brought home from far-away lands where it is never winter, and the big waves roll up on the yellow sands every day of the year.

It made geography very interesting, to see the places on the map where the shells came from. If one was very good about whispering for a whole week, she might be allowed to dust the whatnot and arrange all the shells. Every little girl tried to keep from whispering, you may be sure.

In the window was a yellow canary called

Trill. He sang so loud sometimes that he had to be carried into another room. There were plants in the windows, too, so it did not look much like a schoolroom, but more like a place to have good times in.

And the children did have good times. Some days Miss Maria's mother baked bread. Then it seemed as if always just at lunch time, there was a fresh buttered "rusk" for each one,— yellow, and spicy, and "light as a feather." No one ever made such delicious rusks as Miss Maria's mother.

On rainy days, when the children could not run outdoors on account of bringing in too much mud, Miss Maria opened the drawer of her secretary (as the old desk and bookcase was called), and took out of it a small box. Laura Louise loved this box. It was dark and shining, and had tiny pieces of pearl set into it in the form of flowers and birds and trees and such queer looking men. It had come from China, brought home by that same sailor brother who brought the shells.

In the box were "transfer pictures." They came in long strips that folded up into a little book. Each double page of the book was either filled with tiny pictures, or had a few larger ones on it, or maybe just one big picture. You

could buy transfers any way you wished. Most of those in the "pearly box" had small pictures. That way, you see, one has more of them.

In the same box were a number of small squares of white paper, all the same size. Miss King gave one to each Little Girl, and two or three of the small transfers.

In transfer pictures, you do not see the picture at first, but just a spot of gilt. You cannot even guess what is under it. But you wet this gilt place, and then lay it down just where you want it to be on your white paper. When it has lain there a little while, you take hold of one corner of the transfer and carefully lift it up. And there is the prettiest little picture on the card! It may be a duck, or a little calf, or Mary and her lamb, or a boy rolling a hoop, or anything. You never know.

Every little girl was "collecting" transfer pictures. It was great fun.

Now in such a pleasant school as this, you would not think there could be such a thing as scowls or cross words, would you? But dear me! they seem to be found in places where one would never dream of looking for them. Did you ever notice that?

One day Mabel Wheeler brought to the school an old black locket. It was not pretty; it did not even *shine*, but was dull and rough. But it had two things about it that all the Little Girls liked. It had a ring through which a narrow ribbon could be slipped, to wear around the neck; and — it opened and shut!

Laura Louise wanted the locket. She thought about it all through the Psalm, and the singing, and third reader class. Just the minute recess came, she ran to Mabel and offered all her transfer cards for the locket.

Jenny Gillette wanted the locket, too. She offered *her* cards! "I'll let you wheel my new doll buggy a whole hour besides," she added, as Mabel was holding out the locket toward Laura.

This was too much. Jenny Gillette had the only doll buggy in the village, and every little girl longed to wheel it. So Jenny got the locket too. It often happens that way. But Laura Louise got a poor mark in numbers, because she cried so hard she could not answer the questions.

Jenny Gillette and Laura Louise always walked home from school together, because their houses were side by side. At noon, this time, they walked one on one side of the street and one on the other.

And at night, Laura Louise went home the other way around, where you had to go through a big, roaring sawmill and over a long, narrow bridge. Mother had said never to come that way.

That was the beginning of the trouble made by the black locket. Jenny tossed her curls and fingered the locket, and Laura Louise scowled and did not study her lessons. One day at recess, she snatched the locket off Jenny's neck, and threw it over the fence.

Miss Maria came briskly out to see what was wrong with the Little Girls.

"She snatched my locket!" cried Jenny.

"It would have been my locket if she hadn't coaxed it away with her old doll buggy!" said Laura Louise.

"I didn't!"

"She did!"

Miss Maria rang the bell, which she had in her hand, and the children filed slowly back into the room. Recess was not half over. Laura Louise stayed behind to find the locket. When she brought it into the school room, Miss Maria took it and put it into the secretary.

That evening Jenny Gillette and Laura Louise stayed after the others were gone. Miss Maria

talked to them about the locket, and how foolish and wrong it is to quarrel. It is wicked besides, and grieves the good angels away from us when we allow the bad angels to speak through our mouths. "I think both of you have been at fault in this," she said, "and I hope that you will think it over and come back friends in the morning. The locket is yours, Jenny, but I should prefer that you leave it at home after this. Good night, girls."

Jenny Gillette and Laura Louise felt rather foolish. "I don't care about the old locket — you take it," said Jenny when they reached her gate.

"No, you keep it; I don't want it, really," said Laura Louise.

All at once she didn't want it, *really*. She thought about that afterward, and wondered why she had wanted it at all. She remembered, more than once, when she was tempted to want things that other little girls had, about the black locket that made so much trouble. She found that the best way to be happy was to like what she had herself, and to be glad when other little girls had things, even if she could not have them.

The Hornet's Nest

HORACE and Nelson lived in the country, and a very beautiful country, too, with great fields of corn and wheat, and grand woods with large trees. There were more trees and more woods in that country when Horace and Nelson were little than there are now.

Near Nelson's house there was a maple grove. The small brush had been cut away and stacked up in piles. Nelson thought it a delightful place to play. Horace thought so, too. He came every day to play with Nelson.

Nelson liked very well to have his own way about the games, and to say who should be "it," and who should give the orders and who should obey them. Horace liked to do that, too. So, because it happened that Horace was a little older and a little larger, Nelson often had to give up his way, and do the way Horace wanted.

One day Horace and Nelson found a hornets' nest right across the road from Nelson's house. It was on a low brush heap, and was as large as a milk pan.

There seems to be something in every little boy who sees a hornets' nest that makes him want to punch it open or break it down. A great many little boys, first and last, have tried this, and been sorry afterward; but still they have to keep on, it seems.

"I'll tell you what I'll do," said Nelson. "I'll get the horse blanket, and you tie it with a piece of clothes line over my head and arms, tight, so no old hornets can get inside. Then you lead me right up to the nest, and guide me by saying gee and haw, and I'll walk right up and tramp on that nest, I will!"

"No, you won't! *I'm* going to tramp on it."

"It's my turn to be first chooser!"

"Not for this; I'm going to be it, so you might just as well step around."

This was not pleasant talk from one little boy to another, but so often one hears talk very much like that. Nelson had heard it before, and he was used to giving up, so he said, "Aw, all right," and went after the horse blanket.

Horace went and found a piece of clothes line.

It was a very hot day, and not at all comfortable under the folded blanket, especially when the line was wound tightly round and round and round Horace. He could not move his arms at all. He could hardly breathe. But he was having his own way, so he could afford to suffer a little.

By and by he was all tied up, and ready to start. Nelson led him up close to the brush pile, and then began to direct him, just as they had planned. Horace kept his head, and walked straight forward toward the nest, and planted one stubby boot right down into it.

What happened then is almost too painful to talk about. Such running and yelling I am sure was never seen and heard before on that farm.

The hornets swarmed out, buzzing and angry. It never really pays to stir up hornets. Nelson knew that, and as the black cloud flew out of the nest, he ran toward home.

Horace could not see, and there was no one to say gee and haw, either; but some way he ran straight toward Nelson.

He could not make a very big noise; one can't very well, with two thicknesses of horse blanket

tied over one's head; but Nelson made enough for two boys.

His mother, paring apples in the kitchen, heard the racket, and came out with the paring knife still in her hand. Much more quickly than I can tell it, she ran to Horace, and cut the ropes that bound him. Then she sent him to the barn to take off his clothes.

Poor Horace! The hornets had crawled inside his knee pants, and in spite of the blanket and the clothes line, they were up under his shirt. He was dreadfully stung, and red, angry bunches covered his body. His mother came, took him home, and put him to bed, and there he stayed for several days.

This is the end of the story. I do not know what Horace thought about as he lay in bed, all swollen and smarting and sore; but I have wondered if he might not have decided that sometimes a little boy is just as well off when he does not have his own way!

My Little Brook

MY laughing brook, my singing brook,
   Is brown and clear;
Its shining face, its sparkling look,
Its gurgles in each pebbly nook,
   To me are dear.

Beside its banks I love to play
   From morn till night;
I wade its dancing waters gay,
And come again another day
   With new delight.

On it my ships sail swiftly by,
   A gallant fleet,
While far above it soft clouds lie,
And round it small winds gently sigh
   That it is sweet.

All day it laughs and sings in glee,
   And all night, too;
It is a happy brook, you see;
Its secret it has told to me,
   And I'll tell you.

As low its pleasant song it sings,
   So sweet, so free,
And all along good cheer it brings,
'Tis on its way, as if on wings,
   To join the sea!

"I'm Sorry"

ALBERTA COLTON was a dear little girl, and she lived in a little house on Our Street. There was a wide porch, which was pleasant to play on when the sun was hot. Roses and pinks and lilies blossomed in the front yard, strawberries and raspberries grew in the back yard, and fluffy yellow chicks ran about a little while in the evening over the green grass.

It was just the kind of place, you see, for a little girl to be happy in.

Alberta had a lovely mother and a kind father. But she was like some other little girls.

> Some days she was sweet and sunny;
> Others, she was cross and "funny,"

just like — well, now, do *you* know any little girls like that?

There were other houses on Our Street. Right

across from Alberta's house was another little home, with roses and strawberries and a wide front porch. Miss Ruth Parker, who loved Alberta dearly, lived there. So did Mr. Parker, who called her "Miss Alberta," and gave her cookies to eat. So did Mrs. Parker, who sometimes made little verses for her, like this:

At Our House we are happy,
   At Our House we can smile,
Because Alberta Colton
   Has come to stay a while.

Whenever we are weary,
   Whenever things are queer,
We only need Alberta
   To bring us all good cheer.

Every day Alberta's lovely mother taught her to be polite and pleasant and kind. Her father talked to her, too, and read stories to her from the Bible. And Alberta meant to be a good little girl, but sometimes she forgot.

By and by Alberta's mother became very sick, and her father took her away where she could get well. Alberta went to stay with Mrs.

Mack, next door. Mrs. Mack had a little boy, Willard, so most of the time Alberta was too busy playing to be lonely.

But one afternoon Willard was taking his nap on the back porch, and Mrs. Mack was sewing in the house. Alberta was lonely. There was no one to play with. No one was in sight but Mr. Parker. He was busy, rubbing paint and putty into the cracks on the floor of his porch. When Alberta went up and stood beside him, he only said, "Good afternoon, Miss Alberta," and went right on working. He never even mentioned the cooky-jar.

Then Alberta felt cross, and a naughty thought came into her head. She ran down the steps to the side of the road, and filled her apron with sand and small stones. Then she went back where Mr. Parker was working so carefully to make the porch floor smooth, and threw the sand and stones right down on the wet paint.

Mr. Parker looked very stern. "Take the sand away, Alberta," he said.

"I won't," said Alberta.

"Then you must go away," he said. "No little girl can stay in my yard who acts this way."

Alberta knew that he meant what he said, so

she walked slowly away. "I won't go," she said, but still she went.

It was very quiet. Mr. Parker brushed away the sand, and wiped off the spoiled paint with a cloth. And Alberta walked slowly up and down, up and down, on the sidewalk.

But Alberta was not alone, even though she felt alone, and could not see any one with her. Every little child has a guardian angel, who stays near by all the time, and I am sure a good angel walked back and forth with Alberta that day. I will tell you why.

By and by the ugly frown left Alberta's face, her lips looked sweet and pleasant, and she came quietly up the steps, and onto the porch where Mr. Parker was working.

"Please," she said very softly, "Please, Mr. Parker, I'm — I'm — sorry."

"All right, Miss Alberta," said Mr. Parker laying down his brushes and giving her a good hug. "Now we are friends."

Then he went on working, and Alberta stayed and played till Willard woke up from his nap. She was not lonely any more, nor cross, but the happy, sweet little neighbor folks are always glad to see.

The Invitation

CLARA'S going to give a party,
   And the children all may come,
There'll be tables for the supper,
   And ice cream for every one;
Hide-and-seek beneath the maples,
   Skipping ropes, and balls, and swings,
Boat rides on the shining river,
   And all sorts of lovely things.

Flies the news around our village
   Like a little singing bird,
All the eager lads and lassies
   Homeward bear the joyful word.
Mothers smile, and tell their darlings
   How to act in ways polite.
Little else is talked of, dreamed of,
   For a week from morn till night.

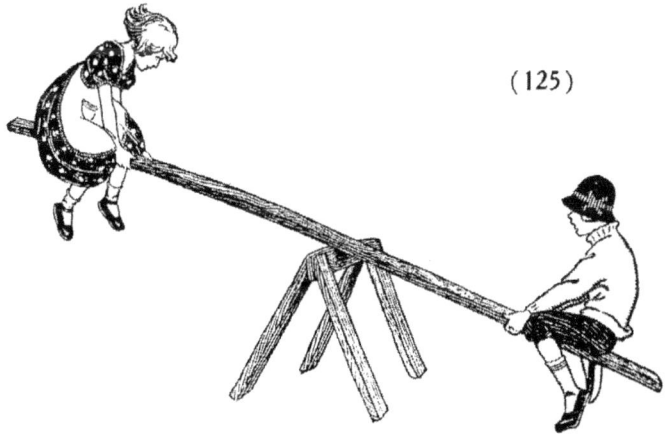

Comes a day when blushing Clara,
    Father walking by her side,
Calls at Our House to invite us,
    Eyes alight with happy pride.
"Will you please," she asks demurely,
    And her words give me a shock,
"Come to party at my birthday
    On next Three-day, Fri o'clock!"

"*Tell It To Jesus*"

KATHERINE-DEAR and Norma-darling and Auntie Pill and father and mother lived at the army post of Camp Hayt on the island of Samar, far, far away in the Pacific.

Katherine-dear was four years old. She had dark-brown eyes and dark-brown curls, and a very loving little heart.

Norma-darling was only a baby, not two years old. If you wish to know how she looked, think of the very loveliest brown-eyed doll you ever saw, for Norma-darling looked like that, only sweeter, because she could *smile*. Some dolls are made, you know, with eyes that open and shut; some have legs that can walk; some even squeak out a few queer-sounding words. But no one can make a doll that can truly laugh and cry and smile.

Auntie Pill was just a dear little brown-eyed girl herself.

The house in which Katherine-dear and Norma-darling and Auntie Pill lived would look strange to you. It was built high up from the ground, for coolness; for it is always hot in Samar. The walls were made of thin strips of wood. There was no glass in the sliding windows, but tiny square "panes" made of thin, flat shells picked up on the seashore. All the houses in Samar had sliding windows with seashells for panes; that is, all the good houses. The poorer homes had woven mats or strips of woven split "bamboo" for windows.

But the roof was strangest of all. It was made of the leaves of the "nipa" palm. It shaded the rooms from the hot sun, but it was not so good at keeping out the rain.

Sometimes there were very dreadful storms at Samar. The wind would blow and blow, harder and harder, and oh, how the rain would pour down! It would come through the roof, and the only way to keep dry was to raise a big umbrella and sit under it, right in the house.

These terrible storms are called *baguios*. They come so quickly that when men whose business it is to watch the weather see a storm coming to Camp Hayt, they send a message to the army people, saying:

"*Baguio coming! Get ready!*"

Three times in a few days, this message came to Camp Hayt: "Baguio coming! Get ready!"

Every time mother had all the beds and chairs and trunks and bureaus drawn together in the middle of the largest room. The pictures and books were piled on top of the beds, and all the food that would spoil by getting wet was stored under them. Large water-proof cloths, called *tarpaulins*, were tied down snugly over all.

Three times the message came; three times mother got everything ready; and three times the baguio did not come.

"I would rather have a baguio than all this trouble," said mother after the third time.

"I think *not*," said father.

The very next day the message came once more: "Baguio coming! Get ready!"

But this time father happened to be away from home, out with his soldiers, and mother did not get ready. And this time the baguio *did* come. Then how mother and Auntie Pill and the servants rushed about the house, shutting doors and

windows, and bringing in all the things that would blow away. But very soon the wind blew so hard that the rain beat in through the walls and windows and began to pour down through the roof.

Then mother took Norma-darling out of her crib and held the big umbrella down close to keep her dry. "What will become of us?" she cried. Her face was very white.

Auntie Pill ran here and there, fast, covering up the food and books, and helping all she could. She was afraid, too, for the wind blew so hard on the house that it shook and rattled; but she only worked faster and faster.

Katherine-dear was too little to work, but she knew something to do to help. She had heard the Bible story of how Jesus said one time to a dreadful storm on Galilee, "Peace, be still," and the wind stopped blowing. And often and often she had sung the sweet words of the song, "Tell it to Jesus, tell it to Jesus." So now she went away by herself into another room and kneeled down and asked Jesus to take care of mother and father and Auntie Pill and Norma-darling, and to keep them all safely.

Jesus hears children pray, and Katherine-dear knew that He had heard her. So in spite of the storm, her little heart was very happy. She ran to tell her mother.

"Jesus will take care of us, mother," she said, patting mother's arm. "I have asked Him to, and I know He will."

"Yes, Katherine-dear," said mother, "and we *will* trust Him."

And Jesus did keep them all safely through that dreadful storm. And though she was a little girl, and all this happened years ago, whenever trouble has come to Katherine-dear since that time, she has remembered how Jesus kept them through the baguio in Samar, and has trusted in His love.

"What is the matter and what is your name?" asked the brisk little girl.

When Norma Was Lost

WHEN Norma Jackson was four years old, she and her father and mother, her sister Katherine and her Auntie Pearl took a long, long journey on a big ship on the Pacific Ocean. They were not going away from America, but coming home, for Norma was born in the far-off Philippine Islands. When they reached America, they lived in a pleasant house on a quiet street near the park in San Francisco. Every Sabbath they went to Sabbath school, and Norma was in the kindergarten.

Now in a large city some little boy or girl gets lost almost every day. So Norma's father taught her to say, when people asked, "What is your name, dear?"

"My name is Norma Elizabeth Jackson, and I live at No. 999 Penelope Street."

Father made a game of it. Sometimes when

Norma ran down the walk to meet him, he would take off his hat, bow very low, and say gravely, "And what little girl is *this?*"

"I am Norma Elizabeth Jackson," Norma would reply, quickly.

"And where does Miss Norma Jackson live?" he would ask, politely.

Then Norma's brown eyes would shine with fun as she said, "I live at No. 999 Penelope Street," and she went in with him at their own front door.

One Sabbath, Katherine and Norma and Auntie Pearl went to Sabbath school on Laguna Street. Then they all went home to dinner with Aunt Vinnie.

When it was nearly dark, they started to walk home. Norma was carrying a "half-moon pie" which Aunt Vinnie had baked especially for her. She was so happy that she could not walk, but ran dancing ahead of Auntie Pearl and Katherine. She did not even notice when they turned off on their own street. They did not notice, either; and when they went into the house, they thought Norma was already there.

But Norma was all alone, and somehow everything looked very strange. It was growing darker, too. By and by the street lamps began to shine. Then Norma began to cry, softly. "Mamma! Mamma!" she called. Then, "Auntie Pill! Auntie Pill!"

But no one saw her or paid any attention.

So Norma cried louder. You would, too. And by and by a bigger little girl, a brisk little girl, came running by.

"What is the matter, and what is your name?" asked the brisk little girl.

"I want my mamma," sobbed Norma.

"Then tell me your name and where you live, quick!" said the bigger little girl.

"My name is Norma Elizabeth Jackson, and I live at No. 999 Penelope Street," answered Norma, still crying.

"All right, I'll send someone to get you," said the careless little girl (I call her careless because she did not take Norma's hand, and lead her home), and away she ran. I am sure if she had had any small sisters, she would not have left dear little Norma crying there alone. But this is a true story, and I must tell it just as it happened. Maybe the bigger little girl was in a great hurry. Anyway, off she ran, pell-mell; but she did stop at No. 999 Penelope Street long

enough to ask, "Does a little girl named *Nora* live here?"

"No," said Auntie Pearl.

"But there is a little girl over on Orange Street, who says she lives here, and her name is Nora, and —"

"Pearl, *where* is Norma?" asked Mrs. Jackson, interrupting the little girl's story. And then all at once they realized that Norma *was not there*.

Then how quickly they ran down the street and on till they came to where Norma was standing by a lamp post, crying, but still holding fast to her "half-moon pie."

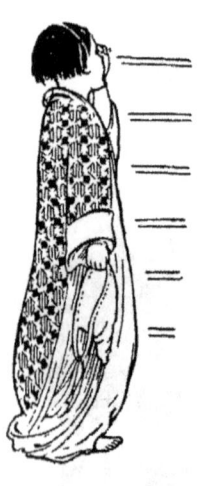

"Norma-darling, *you* know the way home," said mother, and all at once Norma did know. She did not feel lost a bit, and they all walked home as happy as could be. For supper, Norma ate her "half-moon pie," and gave a taste to father and mother and Katherine and Auntie Pill.

When father heard all about it, he said,

"When you're lost again, my sweet,
Make your head direct your feet.
Never cry. Speak plain, and say,
'Will you please show me the way?'"

Whistle, My Lad

WHISTLE, my lad, when there's work to do,
It will make you strong, it will help you through,
    So whistle, my lad, by the hour!
Whistle, my lad, when the task seems long,
You can lighten the hardest task with song.
    In whistling, my lad, there is power.

Mother grows old, but she loves the boy
Who whistles at work, and who sings for joy
    Because there is work to be done.
"It's John," she says, "he will soon be here,
I can tell that whistle from far or near,
    There never was such a good son."

I. H. Evans.

Saying and Doing

"If I had a thousand dollars,"
    Said Beecher in boastful mood,
"I'd take out a hundred this minute,
    I'd pay the tithe first, *I* would.

"And if I had a hundred nickels,
    Shiny and bright and new,
First of all I'd pay ten for tithing;
    That's surely the way *I'd* do.

"But I've only (*you see?*) ten pennies,
    Shabby and brown and small;
So I think I'll not bother to tithe them;
    Really, I need them *all.*"

Let's remember, all we who have pennies,
    And we who have nickels and more,
That God asks a faithful tithing
    Of just what we have in store.

Let others pay tithe of thousands,
    Or of millions, if that may be.
If I am a faithful steward,
    I'll tithe what He gives to me.

Playing Doctor

FATHER MORRIS was a doctor, and Mother Morris was a nurse, so Betty and George thought "playing doctor" the best game of all. George was always the doctor, and Betty was always the nurse.

But a doctor must have someone to visit, and a nurse must have someone to take care of. So it was the most fun when Timmie and Linnie, the Bartholf twins, came to be the "patients."

Timmie and Linnie were little, and Timmie and Linnie were poor, and — this is sad to tell — Timmie and Linnie were often very dirty.

One day Timmie and Linnie came to spend the afternoon. Father had gone to see a little boy who had fallen out of an apple tree and broken his arm, and Mother was helping a neighbor whose little girl had the measles; so the children were all alone.

"Let's play doctor," said George. "I'll be the doctor," he added.

"All right," agreed Betty, "I'll be nurse."

So Timmie and Linnie lay down on the lounge, and Nurse Betty pinned on her white apron, and tied a white napkin over her yellow curls. For the *first* duty of a nurse is to be very clean herself.

"Now, children," she said, "you lie quiet, and I will telephone for the doctor. While we wait, I'll give you a soap shampoo to the face and hands."

Timmie and Linnie did not like this part of the game very well, but the *second* duty of a nurse is to keep her patients clean; so in a few minutes, Timmie and Linnie were scrubbed and rosy.

Ting-a-ling! Ting-a-ling! rang the bell.

"Come in, Dr. George," said Nurse Betty, looking very serious.

"Well, *well, WELL!* What have we here?" said Dr. George, setting down his satchel, taking off his big hat, and looking over his colored spectacles.

"The children have headaches, and they look feverish," said Nurse Betty.

"H'm-'m! Stick out your tongue," said Dr.

Really Trulies 141

George to Timmie, at the same time putting his thermometer (an old one that Father had given him) under Linnie's tongue.

The patients were very quiet while pulses were counted, and tongues examined, and the thermometer was read.

Then Dr. George, looking very wise, said in a low voice to Nurse Betty: "These children are not going to have scarlet fever. They need a tonic. First give a little of the pink tonic, and by and by each may have a big, juicy apple. I'm sure they'll be all right by supper time."

Now George and Betty knew quite well that they were not to meddle with the medicine bottles in neat rows on the shelves in Father's office; but in spite of this they went in and, taking a bottle of pink liquid from the shelf, wet the cork once and put it on Timmie's lips, and once more and put it on Linnie's lips.

"Ow-ow-ow!" yelled Timmie.

"Ouch! ouch! ouch!" cried Linnie.

Dr. George looked at Timmie and Linnie, and then, frightened, at Nurse Betty. For there was a bluish spot, just the size of the cork, that smarted and burned, on Timmie's lips, and another spot just like it on Linnie's lips.

Nurse Betty was frightened too. "It's the 'battery fluid'!" she said. Quickly they put a little thick cream on the burned places to ease the smarting. "We must pray that the Lord will forgive us for meddling, and not let Timmie and Linnie be hurt," they said. So they all knelt down and prayed, and asked to be forgiven, and that no harm might come to Timmie and Linnie. Afterward they gave a juicy, red apple to Timmie and another juicy, red apple to Linnie, and these, as you can easily see, were a great comfort to the patients.

When mother came home, they told her all about it. Mother is the best person in the world to tell when we are in trouble.

"A doctor must *never* make mistakes," said mother, kindly. "But he cannot tell by the color of the medicine or the shape of the bottle, what it is good for. He must study a long time, and even when he has learned about hundreds of medicines, he must always be very careful. I'm sure my little 'Dr. George' will never meddle with Father's medicines again," she said pleasantly.

"I'm sure, too!" said Doctor George.

Dolly Must Go To Bed

Yes, Bess must go to bed,
   For she's been sick all day.
Perhaps it is her head,
   It may be too much play.

She's been so cross, I tried
   To make her rest and sleep;
Her apron strings I tied,
   And let her mop and sweep.

She helped me make the pies,
   The little Honey-dear!
My mother often sighs,
   When I am helping her.

She's lots of care, my Bess,
   She's 'sposed to measles, too!
Now, pet, take off that dress,
   And stop your crying — do.

O Bess, you naughty girl,
    You've spilled your catnip tea;
My head is in a whirl,
    You are too much for me.

Now shut your eyes and sleep,
    And I will sing to you,
My pretty, sweet Bo-peep,
    Shut fast your eyes so blue.

Go to sleep, go to sleep,
    My little Honey-dear,
Go to sleep, go — to — sleep,
    Your mamma is right here.

Now, little sweet, good night;
    I'm very sleepy, too.
My eyes — are — shut — so — tight
    I — can't — see — even — you!

The Picnic

IT WAS early summer time. On the hill which sloped to the south the children had picked wild strawberries more than one sunny afternoon. Wild strawberries are small, and such a deep red color, and oh so sweet! It takes a long time to pick enough to make strawberry shortcake, because so many of them go into your mouth instead of into the pail.

But now the strawberries were nearly all gone, and the raspberries and shining blackberries were ready. Not in the back yard, where *we* pick berries, but in the "clearings" and pastures and woods. There were more berries to pick in those days, and fewer persons to pick them, than there are now.

"We must go berrying," said mother, one day.

"Let's go to-morrow," said father. "Wilson's Woods are full of berries."

"I can help pick," said Jeanne.

"What about the baby?" asked father.

"We'll put a pillow in a bushel basket," said mother, "and his blankets, and he'll be all right. When he's asleep, I'll spread netting over his face to keep away the flies, and he won't know that he isn't in his own crib."

Bright and early the next morning they started, father and mother and Jeanne and little Ruth and baby George. One basket held sandwiches and cookies and bottles of fresh milk; another was fixed into a cozy cradle for the baby. Even Cleve and Fan, the colts, seemed to know that it was a holiday picnic, and pranced along as if they enjoyed it.

Wilson's Woods were ten miles away; but by the time the dew was dry, the colts were turning off the main road into a narrow lane, where the wagon went bump, bump. The lane led to a field that ended in a hill. Once all this land had been covered with a great forest, but now there were only a few large trees, though it was called Wilson's Woods just the same as if the trees had not been cut down long before.

Everywhere there were berry bushes, some small, with their ripe fruit low enough for Jeanne

to reach easily, and others taller than father's head, with long, drooping branches.

"We can easily get all we shall need for winter," mother said, "if we pick fast."

Baby George was asleep. When he was carefully tucked into his basket, which was left in the wagon, and Cleve and Fan were tied where there was plenty of tender grass to nibble, father and mother and Jeanne began to pick. Even little Ruth tried to help at first, but she was soon tired of it.

As fast as father picked all the berries on one bush, he went to another. Mother did the same. "Stay with me, Jeanne," said father, "and empty your cap into my pail. Ruth will stay with mother. Then you won't get lost."

But the children thought it more fun to run back and forth, and not stay just in one place.

So it happened after a while that Jeanne was standing under a tall blackberry bush. There were bushes all around her. It was very still. She couldn't see father or mother or Ruth or the wagon or even Cleve and Fan! For a minute she didn't even *stir*, she was so scared. Then she did what most little girls do when they are lost, she began to cry!

"Father! Father!" she called. But her voice sounded very low and faint in her ears.

"What's the matter, Pet?" called father.

My, Jeanne was surprised! There was father right on the other side of the bush! He knew where his little girl was all the time!

"Why — why — I thought you were *lost!*" said Jeanne.

Father laughed then, you may be sure. But after that Jeanne was careful to see that he didn't get lost again! She stayed close by his side.

By dinner time a number of pails and small baskets were filled with berries. Father found a beautiful place in which to eat. There was a great, smooth, flat rock, by a brook, and near by a bubbling spring with pure water, cold and clear, to drink. Mother spread the food on the rock, and they all sat on the edges to eat. It was great fun, and how good everything tasted!

"Shall we go home now?" asked father. "You mustn't get too tired, you know."

"O, let's stay a little longer," said mother. "The baby is so good outdoors, and Jeanne and Ruth can take their naps on the straw in the wagon bed."

Ruth's curly head was already nodding, and

someway Jeanne felt as if she wouldn't mind a nap as much as usual. When she woke up, father was coming toward the wagon carrying a heavy pail full of berries in each hand.

"Many," said little Ruth, who woke up, too.

"Yes, many," said mother, who was thinking that it would take busy work to put them all into glass jars to-morrow. "I think we have almost enough now," she added, "we'll pick just a few more, and then home we go!"

But it was almost sunset when they went bump-bumping down the lane, and the fireflies were flitting here and there when, tired but happy, they reached home again, and father lifted them one by one onto the "horse block" at the side of the house.

"It was the *nicest* picnic, mother," said Jeanne.

"I think so, too," said mother.

Bernice Irene

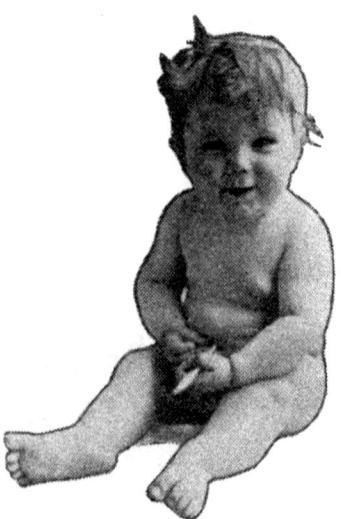

TEN months old is Bernice Irene,
    On our street,
Soft and cuddly, shy yet friendly,
    And so sweet.

All life's long and weary lessons
    Yet to know!
One short word her joy expresses —
    "Oh-h-h! Oh-h-h! Oh-h-h!"

I have loved a hundred babies,
    North and south,
But I never loved such dimples,
    Such a mouth!

All her ways, so mild and gentle,
    Hearts beguile;
There are those would cross an ocean
    For her smile.

Should I have a dozen babies, —
    This is true, —
I should wish them, Bernice Irene,
    All like *you!*

When Jack Said "No"

JACK ROSS lived in the country in Michigan. The land was low and wet and covered with large trees, in those days; for it was a long time ago when Jack was a little boy. Still, he was a lively boy, full of fun, just like little boys who have the same name to-day.

Everybody was poor in that neighborhood, but Jack's father and mother were poorest of all; for they had just come to their new farm. There were eight children besides Jack. They all worked hard, and their clothes were plain and poor, and they had only the simplest food to eat.

But in spite of all this, these children were *rich*. They had a wonderful mother. She is an old lady now, but with such a merry light in her black eyes that it makes you feel good inside just to look at her. Children who went to stay in her house always had a good time. So no matter

what these children didn't have, I think they were rich.

Jack's father was a friendly, social man; but like many other men, he smoked and sometimes took a drink of liquor.

At first there was no town and no saloon near their farm; so all went well. But by and by a little village grew up, only a mile and a half away, and then a saloon was opened, and beer and liquor were sold to all who would buy. The men on the farms nearby would often go to the village at night, and gather in the saloon to visit and drink. Jack's father went, too. Sometimes he came home very late, and often he was very cross the next day.

One night Jack heard his mother crying, and climbing out of bed, he crept to her door and looked. There was his mother, whom he had never seen crying, sitting at the table, with her head bowed on her hands, and sobbing bitterly. Jack could not bear to see his mother cry. Pushing back the pink curtain, he ran to her, and put his arms around her neck.

"Mother, what is the matter?" he asked.

"Jack, will you promise mother just one thing?"

"'Course I will, mother."

Really Trulies 153

"Father has taken to drinking, Jack," said his mother, quietly; "that is why he does not stay at home with us at night as he used to do. Often he is cross to us, and he has dreadful headaches, too. To-day he sold Black Bess, and has paid the money to the saloon, so there will be no money for food or clothes or to pay for yarn to knit the winter stockings. Now I want you to promise me that you will never drink beer or liquor of any kind till you are thirty years old."

Jack knew very well about their lack of warm clothing; for though it was then nearly Thanksgiving Day, he was still going barefooted over the frozen ground. He knew Black Bess had gone, and he loved his mother, so he said,

"I promise you, mother. I will never drink liquor nor spend my evenings in town."

About two years after Jack made this promise, his father took him and his brother Henry to town. They drove up to the hotel, and entered the barroom. The boys had never been inside before. Mr. Ross ordered whiskey for himself and beer for the boys, but both boys refused to drink the beer. Then Mr. Ross drank the beer himself, and ordered cider for the boys.

But Jack would not drink even cider in a

saloon. Leaving the room, he climbed into the wagon, and waited for his father and Henry.

By and by Mr. Ross came out and drove to the mill, where a sack of wheat was ground into flour. For a while he did not speak, but by and by he said: "Jack, I was ashamed of you at the hotel."

"I am sorry, father, but I shall never drink beer or liquor," said Jack.

Mr. Ross said no more. But he thought seriously of what he was doing, and from that day he became a better man.

Jack gained a great victory that day. As he grew older, he still kept his promise not to drink and he never smoked cigarettes or cigars. He became a good and useful man. And Jack's mother was proud of her son, for she knew that whatever he promised, he would do.

Brothers

O LITTLE BROTHER! far across the sea,
Joy of a Christian home, hear now my plea;
A tiny home is mine in far Japan,
Where baby boys must grow as best they can.
Our mothers love us much, but do not know
The way that Better Babyhood should go
In cleanliness and all the ways of health
That are your heritage of untold wealth.
Please send kind teachers soon — do not delay —
To guide our mothers in the better way,
O Little Brother!

Dear Little Brother! you are very sweet
In 'broidered robe, and bib and obi neat;
What fun if we could play — two little boys —
You with all mine, and I with your queer toys,
While near at hand our mothers sat and smiled,
Each filled with gentle pleasure in her child.
But since I may not see you, Toki-san,
I'll help you in whatever ways I can,
And make *my* mother, when she looks at *me*,
Think of *your* needs, across the wide, blue sea,
Dear Little Brother!

They both had thick light hair, which often looked as if it had never had a brush or comb

Two Pennies

ONCE upon a time two little boys went to the same school. One little boy was Freddie Dewitt, and the other was Freddie Hicks.

They both had chubby round cheeks, and round blue eyes, and thick light hair, which for some reason often looked as if it had never had a brush or a comb used on it.

The school that Freddie and Freddie went to was a queer school, you will think. For they were the only little boys in it. There were no little girls either. All the pupils were young people who were getting ready to teach school. So Freddie and Freddie had plenty of lessons, you may be sure, and they had to know the answers to all the questions.

The teacher of these young men and women was a man. He seemed quite an old man to Freddie and Freddie, but really he was not very

old. Often he talked to these young people about certain things that older persons *do* seem to enjoy talking about, such as —

> Wash your face and hands each day
> When you enter school from play,
> Brush your shoes and comb your hair,
> Keep your teeth all clean and fair.
> These are little things, 'tis true.
> But they'll be of use to you
> All life through.

And so on. The thing he talked about more often than any other was that boys should *always* have their hair neatly combed when they came into the school room.

But for some reason Freddie and Freddie never seemed to hear a single word!

Still, Freddie and Freddie had good ears. They could hear even very low whispers, so maybe they did hear a little after all. Anyway when "school called" (as they used to say in those days) one afternoon, Freddie and Freddie came in with their hair wet and smooth and shining. Every lock was in place. They sat down, one in the front seat in one row, and the other in the front seat in

Really Trulies

another row. For some queer reason, the teacher seemed to want Freddie and Freddie right up in front!

All the pupils were in their places, sitting still as still when the teacher came in. The first thing he saw was Freddie and Freddie. Then, "Excuse me a moment, young people," he said, very politely, and left the room.

In just a moment he was back. First he went to Freddie Dewitt. "Hold up your hand!" he said, and dropped into it a big shining penny. For all this was long ago, and pennies were as large as our twenty-five-cent pieces in these days. Then he walked over to Freddie Hicks. "Hold up your hand," he said, and dropped another penny into *his* hand.

This was a queer thing to happen in *any* school as you can easily imagine. Freddie and Freddie did not know what to think. All the young people were looking and wondering, too. But in a minute the teacher was standing behind his desk, smiling very pleasantly.

First he bowed low to Freddie Dewitt, then to Freddie Hicks. "For combing your hair," he said.

Then whenever teacher said:
"Brush the hair upon your head,
Keep your fingers clean and neat,
Shine the shoes upon your feet,
Watch with care your spoken word,"
Fred and Freddie *always heard*.

Each Freddie had a big shining penny.

The Spring

Down in the meadow, by the brook,
In such a pretty, shady nook,
   There is a spring;
Around its edge are grasses tall,
Near by all day the catbirds call,
   And thrushes sing.

It's like a mirror smooth and round,
It's like a jewel in the ground,
   It's like a cup;
The golden sand looks very near,
And there the water pure and clear
   Comes bubbling up.

I lean above the grassy rim,
And dip my little bucket in
   The water cold.
There is no other far or near,
So sweet and good, so pure and clear,
   We're often told.

At evening when I'm tucked in bed,
And stars are shining overhead,
   I like to think
That, stepping very soft and still,
Small creatures from the wooded hill
   Come there to drink!

Tobacco

TOBACCO is a dreadful curse,
It makes good bad, and evil worse;
It takes away a boy's good name,
And brings him only grief and shame.

It picks his pockets, spoils his clothes,
And makes "a chimney of his nose";
It burns, as in consuming fire,
Each noble thought, each pure desire.

It is an outlaw in our land,
Wise men and true against it stand;
"We will not hire," say they, "nor pay
The boys and men who smoke all day."

Therefore no matter what may come,—
At work, or play, or safe at home,—
Tobacco I will never smoke,
Nor on its poison vapors choke.

The Visit

WHEN Janet was eight years old, her mother was very sick, and Janet went to stay with Mrs. Henderson, who lived in Rosewood. Janet had been there once or twice when her mother went with her. She loved the little village, and its tall green trees and its wide streets, and the green hills that rise all around it like the rim of a big bowl. Best of all she loved the pleasant house where Mrs. Henderson lived. She wished that she herself lived in a white house with green blinds, and a long walk with a tall green hedge on each side!

And now she was going to stay with "Auntie Isadore" for she did not know how long — till mother was better, anyway.

"I must be very good," she told herself, on the train, "and always polite, and remember to wipe my feet before coming into the house, and

not to slam the doors, and never to gobble my food. I must not shout 'What?' when Auntie Isadore calls me, and I must never meddle with the things I am not supposed to touch."

Janet shut her hands together tightly as she thought of these things. Father had put her on the train, and had said to the man in the blue coat, "Put this young lady off at Rosewood, Will, and thank you"; then he had told her not to be lonesome, given her a bag of peppermints, and waved good-by as the train pulled out of the station.

By and by she began to look out of the window. The train rushed past trees and barns and houses and horses and sheep and cows. It was great fun for a while, but by and by Janet began to have a little queer feeling inside. Maybe she was hungry! It was only three hours on the train to Rosewood, and at home she never ate between meals,— but a lunch had been packed for her, and she decided to eat it. The peppermints followed. Then she looked out of the windows again, and by and by took a short nap.

After all, three hours is a long time when you are going on your first journey "all by yourself."

But at last it ended, as journeys do. There

was Rosewood, and Mrs. Henderson waiting for her at the station, just as father had waited to say good-by. The big conductor carried out her bag, and helped her down the steps.

It was just as lovely at Mrs. Henderson's as Janet remembered it to be. The white house and the walk with the hedge were as pretty as ever. Now she was to stay here a week, maybe two weeks, maybe three. She ought to feel very happy, but someway she felt a little bit — cross!

Perhaps it was eating between meals; perhaps it was too many peppermints; perhaps it was lonesomeness: anyway she did not feel happy inside, and when Janet did not feel happy inside, she was very apt to show it in her face and the very tone of her voice. She did not like her supper of home-made bread, a pat of fresh yellow butter, and a baked apple with cream. It was very much like her suppers at home, and she wanted something *different* when she was being company.

Auntie Isadore looked at Janet once or twice rather seriously before the time came to say good-night. Then she took her up to the cozy bedroom next her own where she was to sleep.

And when she was undressed, and ready for bed, she talked a little to her.

"I love your dear mother very much, Janet," she said. "I have known her since we were girls, just like you. We went to the same school, and studied our lessons from the same books, and shared the lunches that we brought in shining tin pails. In the summer we played at each other's houses, wading in the brook, picking strawberries and raspberries and blackberries as they came, helping our mothers with the dishes, doing things together whenever we could, because we loved to be together. She was always sweet and pleasant and good. She told the truth always. I could depend on her."

"I know," said Janet, softly.

"She has been my best friend for many years," Auntie Isadore went on. "I love her dearly, and I should like to love her little daughter, too. But I cannot like you, just because you are your mother's daughter. If I love *you*, it must be because you are lovable, because you are pleasant and kind and courteous. I hope you are that kind of little girl, Janet."

Janet was surprised. No one but mother had ever talked to her like that. She had supposed that grown-ups either liked you and did things for you and were "nice," or else they didn't like you, and didn't count. She hadn't supposed that the way children *act* made any difference.

When Auntie Isadore went away, Janet thought for what was a long time for a little girl, over what she had said. And she made up her mind to *be* the kind of girl that Auntie Isadore could love, and that other pleasant persons would love too.

And when, after a week, word came from father that mother was better, and wanted to see her little girl, she was proud and happy when Auntie Isadore kissed her good-by and said: "You must come again, Janet, for it is like having your mother a little girl again to have you here."

There was such a beautiful doll with rosy cheeks.

Beth's Happiest Christmas

BETH was sad. There was to be no Christmas tree at their house this year. She was only eleven years old, but she knew that there was very little money for presents of any kind, just as well as if she had been twenty.

Dear father had been very sick a long time. Now he was gone, and their money was nearly used up. "We ought to be thankful for this little house," said mother, "and that you children are well and have enough to eat, and that I have a place to work."

Still, it was hard to think of the things in the shop windows, all bright and glittering, and not want some of them! Beth knew that she was too big for dolls; but — there was such a *beautiful* doll, with rosy cheeks, and light brown curls, and eyes that opened and shut!

She couldn't have it, and there was no use thinking about it. But there wouldn't be any wagons or sleds or picture books or toys or anything that one likes so well to see standing at the foot of a tree, or to pull out of one's stocking on Christmas morning.

"We can be happy just the same," said mother bravely.

Mothers are always brave. Mothers are like that.

Beth missed her dear father; but though she was only a little girl, she knew that mother missed him more. Mother missed him all the time. Yet it was mother who was smiling and cheerful, and Beth who was scowling and sad.

"I don't see how we can be very happy," said Beth. "Jenny and Maud and Alice are all going to have trees, they say, and all kinds of things on them. They always do. They are making things for each other, too, and their houses are just *full* of secrets!"

Beth sighed again. Secrets are half the fun of Christmas.

"Cheer up, dear," said mother. "I'll put on my thinking cap, and see if we can't plan a few things for Christmas. You help grandmother with Esther and Bob and Frances to-day, and to-night when I come home, I'll see what we can do."

Really Trulies 171

That was secret number one, for Beth knew that mother would think of a way.

When supper was over, and the children were in bed, mother and Beth sat down by the kitchen table. On it there was a pile of magazines and papers, and the box of pretty cards which they had been saving for a long time.

"You can make three lovely books, for one thing" said mother, "one for Esther and one for Robert, and a cloth one for little Frances."

"That'll be *three* things," said Beth.

Mother had two books, with stout red covers and strong backs. Inside there were only lists of names, and by taking out some of the pages, they would make good scrapbooks.

"These are just the thing for Esther and Robert," said mother. "You will need to be very careful when you cut out every other page, to keep the edges straight, but if you take pains, they will look just as nice as if they had been bought on purpose. In these papers are dozens of pretty pictures, and in this box I have ever so many stories and verses that have been printed in your Sabbath school papers. All these will be lovely to paste in the books. You know the stories that Robert likes, and you can put those in his

book, and the ones that Esther likes best can go in hers."

By this time, Beth's eyes were shining like stars. She could hardly wait to begin. She would have as much fun trimming the edges of the pictures neatly, and arranging the pictures and verses on the pages, as Esther and Robert would have afterward.

The book for little Frances was to be made of cambric, which cost only a few pennies a yard. The pages were stitched firmly together at the back, and the edges were to be "pinked"— that is, cut with a pinking iron into tiny, fluted scallops. All the pictures of kittens and chickens and cows and little dogs and dollies would go in this book, of course.

Beth's house was full of secrets, too, after that evening. She amused the children for hours at a time by reading them the old stories in the papers, and was careful to see which Robert liked best and which ones Esther loved. When the children were busy, she carefully cut out the verses and stories, and pinned them together. In the evening she pasted them into the books. She could not paste very many at a time, because she must make them lie down flat, and pat the

Really Trulies

edges down all around every picture so they would stick.

Sheets of wrapping paper were saved, ironed out smooth, and laid carefully between the pages, so they would not stick together; then a thin board was laid over the pasted leaves, and the flat-irons piled on it, to weight it, and make the pages dry without wrinkles.

After a few evenings, Beth's pages looked very neat and pretty indeed. "Do you think the children will like them?" she asked. She always called Esther and Robert and Frances "the children."

"They'll be sure to like them," mother said. "I like them, myself."

When the books were finished, Beth made a gray kitten and a white bunny for Frances, of pieces of cloth that mother found in her bag. The gray kitten had black button eyes and black "whiskers," and the bunny's eyes were pink; his ears were pink inside too. "They look just fine," said mother.

And after that there was pop corn to pop and make into balls, and candy to pull and pull and pull, till it was light colored, and each piece just the right thickness. Then it was cut into

small bits, and each piece rolled in cornstarch and wrapped in oiled paper. The hickory nuts that the children had gathered in the fall were brought down, and some of the meats were put into "hickory nut candy," which was cut in tiny squares. Every day and every evening Beth was busy, and every day and every evening she was happy.

At last the great night came, and Beth had her part in filling the stockings. It was such fun! There were a few bundles that she had not seen opened, but she knew what was inside,— a pair of stout shoes for Robert, a pretty woolen dress for Esther, and a warm knit hood and jacket for little Frances.

"If I don't see them, they will be as much a s'prise to me as to the children," she told her mother.

Mother smiled. "The dear child," she thought, "she isn't thinking about herself at all."

And that was one of mother's Christmas presents, and the best one she could ever have! But grandmother and Beth and Esther and Bob had a secret too, and there was a pair of warm gloves in mother's stocking.

You know how hard it is to sleep on Christmas

morning. Long before it is light, your eyes fly open, and you just can't wait to see what is in your stocking! Beth and Esther and Robert and even little Frances were wide awake very early that Christmas morning, and out of bed in a jiffy! Queer it is that way about getting up only on Christmas!

There was no more sleep that day for anybody!

Beth's stocking was not empty! She had known, of course, that there would be tiny boxes covered with bright paper, and filled with the candy she had helped make. There would be popcorn balls, too, wrapped in oiled paper; but she had not thought of anything else. But mother had thought, and grandmother. There was a dress like Esther's, and a pair of warm knit gloves, and a beautiful book with a blue cover—a big book, that told a lovely story all about a family that lived in the days of Martin Luther. Beth liked it especially because it was large and rather fine print. She had only a few books, and one gets through a book so quickly, if the print is large!

"Mother, this has been my happiest Christmas," said Beth when the happy day was over.

"Our happiest days are always the days when we try to make others happy," said mother.

God's Promises

THE Saviour has promised to help me,—
  I read it right here in His Word,—
And pledges more sure or more steadfast
  By mortal ears never were heard.

In the hour of temptation and danger,
  He says, I will hold fast thy hand,
And keep thee, and make thee a blessing
  To souls needing light in the land.

Sometimes I'm afraid in the darkness,
  And faint at the tempest's loud roar;
But when I remember, "I'm with you,"
  Fear goes, and I tremble no more.

He has promised forgiveness for sinning,
  Sweet peace 'mid the world's wild alarms;
And no matter what happens, His children
  Have 'neath them His unfailing arms.

What more could He promise to give them?
  What comfort, or joy, or delight?
Forgiveness, and "keeping," and power,
  And homes in the mansions of light!

TEACH Services, Inc.
PUBLISHING

We invite you to view the complete
selection of titles we publish at:
www.TEACHServices.com

We encourage you to write us
with your thoughts about this,
or any other book we publish at:
info@TEACHServices.com

TEACH Services' titles may be purchased in
bulk quantities for educational, fund-raising,
business, or promotional use.
bulksales@TEACHServices.com

Finally, if you are interested in seeing
your own book in print, please contact us at:
publishing@TEACHServices.com
We are happy to review your manuscript at no charge.

www.ingramcontent.com/pod-product-compliance
Lightning Source LLC
Chambersburg PA
CBHW070552160426
43199CB00014B/2475